Into the Heart of the Beloved

A Romance with the Divine

Anamika

Into the Heart of the Beloved

A Romance with the Divine

Anamika

Published by:
Mountain Cat Productions
2250 King Court #18
San Luis Obispo, CA 93401
805.541.2773
MountainCatProductions.com

Cover Design by Lynda Rae

ISBN, print ed. 0-9755546-1-1
First Printing 2006

Library of Congress Cataloging-in-Publication Data

Anamika, Into the Heart of the Beloved, A Romance with the Divine/ - 1st ed. 2006920539

TABLE OF CONTENTS

DEDICATION

To My Beloved,

You are my devotion, you are my heart, you are the reason that I exist. You are everything to me. There is nothing that means more to me than you. I exist because of you, for you and through you. There is nothing else.

8-Into the Heart of the Beloved

PROLOGUE

Infinite One, join me with you.
My heart aches at the separation
and dances in joy at the union. – Yeshua

If the Nazis came to the door what would I do? This question haunted my childhood. Would I faint? Would I run and hide? Would I resist even if it meant losing my life?

These questions were understandable given that I grew up in a Jewish household not too long after World War II. However, the intensity of my feelings surrounding this quandary and my desperation to know the answer seemed strange. There was no history of violence in my childhood. My family enjoyed a comfortable upper-middle class, Oyster Bay Cove, New York existence. We valued and practiced kindness. So, my obsession with this Nazi issue had to come from somewhere else.

In attempting to answer these questions, I would conjure up various scenarios. In some, possessing super human strength, I defeated the Nazis' advances. In others, I bravely faced death at the hands of my captors. In yet others, I quaked in terror at the sight of their hard black boots and threatening guns. After each of these ruminations I would be left in a state of great agitation and unrest because I truly didn't know what I would do if confronted in such a way. And so, the quandary continued.

Years later, as I reached through the veils of time, a vivid recollection of a "prior" life made clear the reason for my childhood obsession with the Nazis. Finally, what seemed like an answer emerged. I was a fifteen year old boy in Eastern Europe and one day the Nazis did indeed knock on the door. Although my stomach clenched as terror coursed through my veins, I opened the door and strategically positioned myself in such a way that my body offered what protection it could to shield my family. Courageously, I stood tall before the Nazis, lying to them that my family was not at home. I desperately hoped that the soldiers would believe my ruse and move on.

Instead, they viciously grabbed me and brutally clubbed me to death. Even after my skull was broken, they continued to pummel and kick me. My spirit hovered over my lifeless body in shock at what had happened, watching helplessly as the Nazis stormed the house. They dragged my struggling younger sister, parents and grandparents into the street, and literally threw them in a filthy truck to be hauled off to a concentration camp.

10-Into the Heart of the Beloved

I was devastated beyond description. I had failed in my mission to protect those I loved most and I had failed to defeat the forces of darkness. In an attempt to rectify the situation, my spirit made a desperate effort to re-inhabit my brutalized body. Relatives in spirit turned me around and drew me toward the light, away from my earthly existence. My heart was heavy. I had been determined to be a force of good, believing that it was my mission to save the world and fight the darkness.

From somewhere in the ethers a gentle soothing voice began to speak. *It is not necessary to win that fight. Forgive yourself for not being able to do what you thought you should. Winning a fight is not important. What is important is that you forgive yourself. In so doing, you will attain a profound level of acceptance in which you don't have to be other than who you already are.*

I realized that I was being offered the opportunity to blend with the light and know serenity. I had felt that I was an utter failure because I had not been strong enough to accomplish what I had thought to be right. The comforting voice continued. *Who says you should have been able to defeat the soldiers? Who are you to judge yourself so? Who says that your limited perspective is the only reality? How do you truly know? You can only find out if you forgive yourself and embrace a state of acceptance.*

"I can't do that," I protested. "Some things are just unforgivable. I wasn't able to save my family and help defeat the forces of darkness. I need to go back to Earth to fulfill this mission and I cannot rest until I do."

As you wish. However, if you want to defeat the forces of darkness you will need a very powerful gift, one that is larger than all of the darkness itself.

"Excellent," I exulted. "When do I begin?"

It will require many years of life to reach a level of maturity sufficient to handle this gift. You must not distort it, engage in a fight, or misuse it. You will come to learn that the acceptance of yourself as you are, including both the darkness and the light, is actually what you are seeking, not the conquering of the dark. However, you'll need to discover this for yourself.

You're going to forget this conversation for a time. You will not remember the gift I am giving you or anything about our interaction until you are able to transcend self-judgment sufficiently. When you open to who you are you will remember. So be it.

Of course, just as the voice said, I remembered none of this. My life was consumed by a nameless quest spurred by a nameless angst. It was a desperate search for something that would relieve the ache and make me feel whole. Certainly there were days, even years of pleasure, accomplishment, and learning. By all accounts, I was extremely successful. Yet, something was missing.

A consuming yearning, a longing beyond all things persisted. Usually I placed the focus of this longing on a man. If I could just find the right man, not the one I was currently with, but that ultimate soul mate life partner, the One, then I could have the thirst quenched and the pain lifted.

My search for this love led me all over the planet. I explored high rocky terrain and eerily silent desert. I delved deeply into my psyche, fearlessly searching, questioning, and probing. Stopping at nothing, leaving no stone unturned, I was relentless.

Despite the many insights accumulated through the search, the gaping black hole in my soul persistently haunted me. Where is my man? When will we meet? Why am I here? What is my mission?

A dramatic turning point finally occurred when I met an extraordinarily gifted trance channel named Mataare through whom I received the life-changing gift of ongoing dialogue with the Ascended Masters. Over many years of speaking with them, every belief I had was challenged. Every truth I had held as reality was exposed as fallacy. I was required to strip naked my psyche, relinquish entirely the self I had thought was me. The Masters helped remove my shrouds of self-deception to discover my real self.

Perhaps some go through this gracefully. I am sorry to say I was not one of those. I felt tortured, manipulated, controlled and confused. I pleaded, demanded, raged, bargained, ranted, raved and sobbed my way through. I was certain that if only I had the right man I would be just fine. Then, I would have that consummate love. I thought my search was for a soul mate, for a purpose, for enlightenment. In truth, it was a search to know and accept myself.

This is the story of how my illusions gave way to miraculous grace during a certain period of my life many years ago which involved significant change. Even though further change of far greater significance to me has occurred since, the phase of my life described in these pages delineates a vital piece of the spiritual journey, so I offer it here. While my story is distinctly personal, it is really the story of the human journey, the story of us all. May my quest and revelations assist the divine communion within your own heart to blossom into an ever more passionate love affair.

CHAPTER 1

THE LATE BLOOM

The mission of the light is simply this:
all souls of this world who wish to partake of their
largest destiny shall experience the fullness of their
life force. - Chief Great White Eagle

I should have been on top of the world. By age 36, it seemed that I had reached the pinnacle of my career and personal life. To prove this to myself, I took stock and made a list of everything that I had achieved that I had valued as important.

My list went as follows: I had been involved in the personal growth movement for twenty years. I had graduated from Wellesley College with a B.A. in Psychology, then had gone on to two alternative, self-designed graduate school programs, first to earn a Masters Degree in Psychology and then a Ph.D. as well. Then, I had gone further with my education for four more years and graduated from the Barbara Brennan School of Healing.

At nineteen, before graduating from college, I had begun my counseling practice based mostly on the gifts with which I had been born. Again, taking stock, I listed these gifts: I was able to feel people's emotions, hear their thoughts and perceive their aura. I somehow had an ability to transmit potent energies that catalyzed spontaneous shifts of consciousness in people. I could somehow "read" their soul's lessons and know their deepest motivations and desires. I discovered the names of my gifts: telepathy, empathy, intuition, clairvoyance, clairaudience, clairsentience, mediumship, channeling, direct knowing and energy transmission.

Using these gifts, I had built a successful and prosperous psychotherapy/ energy healing practice in Lexington, Massachusetts. Over the years, I had worked with thousands of clients and workshop participants and had traveled the world leading seminars. By 36, financially I was in the top 1% of women on the planet.

Equally important to me, I was involved with a caring and succesful man who wanted to marry me and I lived in a cozy house with my wonderful Golden Retriever. My list ended with the fact that I had achieved everything I could and that I seemed to be a good person.

This list left me cold and entirely dissatisfied. It did not touch the place inside of a persistent feeling that something was missing Not only was something missing, but whatever it was seemed to be the most important thing.

In reviewing my life I realized that I had felt a yearning even as a child from as early as I could remember. Since the day I was born, I had been searching for that something. I was looking for an inner feeling of fullness, an overwhelming love and an explosive radiant passion that seemed to forever elude me. Instead of this love, deep inside I was tormented by an disconnected aloneness. It was like a cold wind blowing through my soul with gusts of meaninglessness, longing and despair. I yearned for the warmth of an imagined sense of connectedness, oneness and union that would fill my soul.

This angst persisted despite having two loving parents and four siblings. My mother and I shared a powerful bond in particular, which we both considered a special relationship. We had communicated perfectly with a mere glance or a knowing look from the start. We understood each other's thoughts and feelings to the detail. We were psychically attuned with an unshakable feeling that we had known each other for eons. Even as an infant I felt that I was her mother as much as she was mine. It was as if we were one soul.

Yet, despite our extraordinary affinity, and as much as I valued and relied on her love as a foundation, I needed something more. I had a hole in my soul that neither she nor my highly developed awareness could assuage. While my precocious maturity had succesfully precluded the need for normal socialization as a child, now it seemed that it had served to magnify my truer need for a deeper kind of communion.

So at 36 when my life appeared on the outside to be so successful, the feelings of angst inside became overwhelming and acute. Unable to either understand or solve my dilemma, I was convinced that what I lacked was the right man and my true mission. I believed that the physical presence of my real lover, not the one I was with, and clarity about my life purpose would fill the emptiness inside me.

Searching for answers and craving healing balm, I turned outside of the conventional world of psychology. It held no answers, as my problem did not seem rooted in my relationships with mommy, daddy or other. Not knowing where else to turn, I approached psychics, healers, mediums and mystics who I naively thought might have a clue as to where and when I would meet my soul mate and as to the nature of my mission.

This path proved to be a gut wrenching roller coaster ride of wild swings. Each time I thought that I was getting closer to answers, my hopes would rally. Then, they would then be dashed by devastating sorrow as the predictions inevitably proved to be false. Gradually, disillusionment began to outweigh my desperation for answers. I became disgusted and ceased consulting others about these questions. Of necessity, I gave up trying.

In the midst of this despair, my trusted friend Gabriella called in a state of great excitement. Breathlessly, she informed me that Paul McClain, a world class trance channel, was coming back to Boston. Assisted by her own reading with him, she went on to say that he channels your own personal Spirit Guides as well as all of the Ascended Masters. She was adamant that he was exceptionally gifted.

Despite the new "no consulting" policy I had developed due to my prior experiences, I felt compelled to go see him and at once. My impassioned response to this new situation surprised me to such a degree that I overrode my previous policy and set up a reading.

On the day of the appointment, I was unnervingly excited. This was despite a large degree of skepticism that warred with my thwarted, but escalating hopes. My logic argued, "What are you so nervous about? This is just another medium, one more person who channels. You've been to many of these types. He probably won't be any better than the rest!" However, I was surprised to find that I was shaken to the core. My entire body was vibrating with anticipation and fear. I sensed that this time would be different. I hoped against hope that finally my two burning questions might actually be answered.

Driving to the hotel for the reading, all of my worst fears rampaged in cacophonous disarray. I fantasized the Guides coldly reprimanding me when I asked about my soul mate and my mission. "You have no soul mate. You're going to be alone for the rest of your life. Furthermore, you have no mission. So just get used to that!" This imagined response certainly said a lot about the rattled state of my nerves.

With these depressing thoughts as companions, I entered the hotel and approached Paul's suite with the grace and enthusiasm of a robot. Mechanically knocking on the door, I awaited what I believed could only be the inevitable demise of every hope and aspiration I had ever held dear.

After what seemed to be an eternity, the door opened and there stood Paul. I was shocked. Somehow, his appearance was all wrong! I was seized by the irrational conviction that somehow he was supposed to look differently.

He was an unprepossessing man of 5'8", with creamy light brown skin, and of African-American and Cherokee heritage. His shoulder length black hair was pulled back in a ponytail. He had a slightly plump body with wide-set dark eyes which gazed at me blankly. He seemed to be drifting in and out of his body. Somehow it didn't seem that this seemingly unfocused and disoriented man could possess the key to my destiny, I thought dismayed.

To cover my gloomy air and mask my nervousness, I decided to put up a brave front. I marched into the room in a brusque manner, as if paying an official visit, as if I were indeed in charge of the situation. Paul's initial blankness seemed to grow into discomfort as if in response to my impersonal entrance. Strangely, it seemed that my very presence was unusually disconcerting to him, I mused, feeling any slim thread of hope slipping away.

Paul indicated that I follow him into the hotel bedroom. The shades were drawn and I could barely see him in the darkened room. Two chairs had been carefully placed face to face next to a small table which held a tape recorder and a burning candle. He motioned for me to take a seat. "I will be going into trance," he said routinely. "I want you to take off your shoes, stretch and sigh and then chant seven ohms along with me. While you are chanting the ohms I will slip into a trance. Then your Guides, undoubtedly some of whom will be the Ascended Masters, will come through and speak with you."

I immediately panicked. "What is this, a séance?" I argued with myself as I fought the urge to bolt from the room. "Take off my shoes? This guy is supposed to answer the burning questions on which every moment of my future happiness depends and I can't wear my shoes?" I ranted inwardly. I was now even more certain the whole effort was doomed.

"Get a hold of yourself!" another part of me demanded as I made an unsuccessful effort to be more rational. My mind had a will of its own. It went on, "If this guy were a real channel, the energy would just come through automatically and he'd start talking. Why doesn't he just start talking like he's supposed to? What's with the seven ohms?"

For some reason, chanting seven ohms was even worse than taking off my shoes. "These instructions are preposterous and excessively ritualistic. Will the next thing he wants be that we jump up and down and sing *Hallelujah*? I can't do this!" I moaned to myself.

Desperate for a measure of reassurance and sanity as I seemed to be losing my grip, I continued my silent monologue, "Well, perhaps this is what one is required to do to be a full trance channel. How do I know? The other people I have been to were psychics or conscious channels. Gabriella had informed me that this guy leaves his body and goes so far away that he has no recollection of what has transpired. He can even channel Guides who speak in their native tongues, languages with which he had no familiarity. If he is that remarkable, maybe the seven ohms are necessary after all." Pleased and reassured by my self-proclaimed shrewd analysis of the situation, I took off my shoes and did as Paul had instructed.

Right before he slipped into trance, he looked at me in a very different manner than before. It was as if his eyes were looking through me seeing something that was invisible. His look was penetrating and inquiring, "Don't I know you?" He seemed to be scrutinizing my soul and I felt more exposed than I had ever before.

His visual probing lasted just a moment. Then, he closed his eyes and as his breathing deepened his body began to slump in the armchair. Odd sounds emanated from him periodically as the air in the room softened palpably and became highly charged as if the fabric of our surroundings were shifting.

Gradually, I sensed a presence enter Paul's body and adjust itself to his form. The shape of his face and body were undergoing such a transformation that his rather round androgynous features were becoming much sharper and more boldly defined. It was as if he were becoming a different person.

By now I was quivering with anticipation. I felt a strong recognition of the new presence before me whose gentle compassion put me at ease. For the first time that day I felt calm, safe and at peace.

Responding to the new presence, Paul's body gradually adjusted itself to assume a more upright position. He opened his eyes and a soothing voice with an Italian accent began to speak.

Greetings, dear friend. I am happy to come here. I am called Francesco d'Assisi. You might know me as Saint Francis of Assisi. It has been several centuries since you and I have seen each other.

Your soul is very old, very wise and very sensitive. Your life is one of service. Whenever that is your primary focus you find yourself happy. Ones such as you can be extremely vulnerable to what occurs on Earth.

The consciousness of humanity is evolving, but the environment on Earth is not yet nurturing to the spirit. The path of true fulfillment doesn't come from your worldly accomplishments, but rather from your inner spiritual nature. You understood this a long time ago, but you don't understand why this has not brought you a romantic partnership, a mission and everything else you have wanted.

You might look at yourself as the late bloom. When the other flowers fade, the late bloom shines and becomes special. You are not far from what you are looking for, Beloved.

I was trembling as Francesco was addressing my concerns directly. How did he know all about my desire for a soul mate and a mission? Moreover, why would a Saint speak with me? Somehow, it wasn't only his words that spoke to me. His presence emanated a kindness and a tender acceptance that was far beyond anything I had ever known. It was as if he were cradling me in his arms against his heart. I felt that he knew me better than I knew myself. He accepted me compassionately and knew my dreams, my desires, and the concerns of my soul. On some profound level I had come home. Nothing appeared the way I thought it should, but somehow that ceased to matter.

All of these thoughts and impressions took only a moment. There was a long silent pause in which Paul's body began to slump again. During this pause, I felt the gently soothing energy of Francesco depart. Gradually, I sensed another presence occupying Paul's body who was strongly masculine and earthy.

Again Paul's body adjusted itself to an upright position. The entity rubbed his eyes, pulled the rubber band out of Paul's hair and shook his head vigorously to loosen the ponytail. Then he grunted, looking around the hotel room. I was amazed at the change in Paul's appearance. Now he seemed squat, with a large belly and jowly face. Incredibly, he seemed to be wearing a Native American headdress. When he began to speak it was with a thick, gravelly voice:

This room is such a little box! Greetings friend, I am very happy to come here. I am called by a name that does not translate into your language. I could be called Great White Eagle; I am a Chief.

I began to feel a pressure in the center of my chest and a swirling around my heart. "What's happening to my heart?" I blurted out.

It is Yeshua who is working on your heart. Yeshua is the man the Romans later called Jesus, but Yeshua is his ancient Hebrew name. He is one you have spent a great deal of time with.

This seemed downright impossible. I had always rejected any notion of the religious figure Jesus. I felt no need for a savior and he had no relevance to my life. In addition, I had always found the very sound of the name Jesus to be hard and grating. It had never occurred to me that I might have known a presence by the name of Yeshua. This name sounded melodious and resonant. Surprised that I had any desire to speak with him, I heard myself asking, "Can Yeshua speak with me?"

Certainly, and not only him. Many other Masters who are part of the Great White Brotherhood have concern for those in this world who are reaching for the light. We exist near this dimension for the purpose of making it easier for people who seek to surrender into the embrace of the Mother-Father-God. The mission of the light is simply this: all souls of this world who wish to partake of their largest destiny shall experience the fullness of their life force.

The Chief paused and took a long breath. *I love you more than you understand.* His words were filled with great emotion. *It is hard for me to leave you.*

As he spoke, I felt a delicious warmth penetrating the place of yearning within me. *It has been a long time since we have met. But when I go, we will be together in a different way. Go with the Great Spirit, and stay close to your sacred path.*

As he was leaving Paul's body, he appeared before me for a moment as a huge being of golden white light radiating the most beautiful glow I had ever seen. I gasped, overcome with awe and longing as I was lifted up and drawn into his light. I found myself sobbinb as pain welled up and tears of gratitude spilled down my cheeks. This is it! This is the love I have been looking for and I don't want it to ever end!

His love had captivated me and I was utterly transfixed. But gradually, the Chief's light faded. Yet despite its disappearance, I maintained my euphoria. Suddenly, with a lurch and a start, Paul came out of his trance and was unceremoniously plunked back in his body with no recollection of anything that had transpired, just as Gabriella had foretold.

As his eyes came into focus, Paul noticed that I was in the throes of my ecstatic experience. For a brief moment he exhibited none of the initial awkwardness as he beheld me. His eyes clearly showed that he too was was profoundly moved. Years later he told me that at that moment he became certain of the deep, lasting connection between us that he had sensed when he first opened the hotel door. He said that our connection had been there for eons and at some point we had been the same soul, which subsequently divided. In our divided state we had been together consistently in many different kinds of relationships throughout the centuries.

The eternal bond I felt at that moment was not yet with Paul personally, but with the beings he had channeled. I didn't realize that he personally was also to be an integral part of my journey as well as the Masters in spirit who spoke through him.

CHAPTER 2

Risking Trust

For you right now God is "Source"
but it's not going to stay that way.
For you God will become "My Beloved." – Constance

Something changed in me after that first session with the Guides. I was consumed by the desire to constantly feel the depth of the passion and delicious love they had awakened in me. Experiencing that love confirmed that my yearning and quest had not been insane, nor worse yet, in vain. I now had a reference point and a name for what I had been seeking. Although my life was full and busy, I could think of nothing else but the chance to be with the Guides again.

While the weeks and months passed, I began to realize that the love I had experienced with them had always been inside of me, but I had touched it in smaller doses and only rarely. They had given me a larger dose, but it was the same love I was craving because somewhere and somehow I had known it.

It gradually dawned on me that I had always had a connection with these Guides, and in fact they had always been my best friends. They were the ones who had been silently whispering to me from within. With a gentle pressure, their unseen force had guided my movements and choices. They had consistently confirmed my sense of inner knowing. When I had become indecisive or confused, it was their loving influence that impressed me as to where to go and what to do.

As a child, I called this force Nature. I found hints of that something, that Nature, in moments of solitude. When I was alone among the tall oaks in the woods surrounding our house, I would blend with their nameless presence. Lying on my back on the sand by the ocean shore, I would fall upward into the sky, expanding through the clouds into infinity.

I wasn't aware of Nature all of the time. Often it seemed I was acting on my own volition like other people seemed to do. When Nature came to me, it would make its presence known by a great feeling of expansiveness in which

I was quite empathic. I could sense other people's feelings and telepathically read their thoughts. Nature was so attuned to me that it seemed prescient. It was as if it knew what I needed before I did. Because of Nature, I seemed to possess an awareness of other dimensions of reality. Somehow I knew that there was more depth and possibility around than was immediately apparent. For some reason, I was born with access to these other dimensions which informed and guided me.

I think that it was Nature that provided the contrast between my unsettled feelings and the beauty that I sensed to be my destiny. It was as if Nature was constantly reminding me that there was more abundance to life than what this world was offering the young child that I was. This pain was Nature's gift to insure that I would not compromise or settle for less and that I would fulfill my human potential.

With Nature's guidance, I was driven in a quest for some state of love to which I could not give name. It was not the usual human emotion of love that I sought, for I had no lack of that. It was a more expansive state of love that had grabbed my attention.

I sensed that Nature offered a love so much larger and more profound than what I was experiencing. I wasn't content with the limited access I had. I wanted it in its entirety. I craved an explosion inside of its delicious, powerful essence. I yearned to dissolve in its ecstatic, boundless, creative passion.

Given this cosmic preoccupation, being on Earth was like being conscripted to a trivial and tedious play that I knew too well. There was no mystery, no frontier at this stage. It was yet to come I hoped. I couldn't understand why I was required to conduct my affairs at a snail's pace when I was capable of so much more. Sensing something better coming, I had faith that the last act of this play held the promise of magnificent resolution. This potentially fulfilling destiny was my companion, always counseling patience to my impetuous eagerness.

In that first reading, the Guides had reached through veils of despair and grabbed my heart and soul. Miraculously, I didn't feel alone anymore. In finding them, I felt I had come home and found my long lost family, my dearest friends. The exhilarating passion I felt with them was what I had always imagined I would feel with a man. It was the great love for which I had been searching.

Chief Great White Eagle's energy in particular was direct and potent, like liquid gold pulsing through my veins. Through his embrace, I felt all of creation dancing within me in ecstatic lovemaking, all of me pulsing and tingling with wave after wave of exultation and rapture.

What remained of the deep abyss of aloneness and separation inside was now less tolerable than ever. Craving that great love as my constant companion, I determinedly vowed that I would do whatever it took, even walk through fire, to have this love always.

As I made this vow, it was just as well that I didn't know the arduous challenges that lay ahead. Had I known, I'm not certain I would have possessed the necessary fortitude and commitment to carry on. My rapturous experience with the Guides proved to be a sneak preview, a tantalizing taste of a promised land that awaited me while I slogged through a wilderness of despair and suffering.

Unbeknownst to me, my progress would require that I relinquish firmly entrenched and enduring beliefs and self-created identities. I was riddled by a lack of self-worth on the one hand and arrogant superiority on the other. Both of these extremes seemed to be the problem. My quest necessitated a ruthlessly self-examining odyssey in which I would have to become aware of aspects of myself which frightened and repulsed as well as pleased and delighted me. I didn't realize that to enter the embrace of divine love required an ever deepening acceptance of all of me, including the extremes.

I became aware of one such uncomfortable part when after a reading Paul spontaneously and mistakenly called me Alexandra. We were both startled and surmised it meant something significant. He went back into trance so that we could ask the Guides. They informed me that I was not Alexandra but Alexander as in Alexander the Great and that Paul had been my best general and closest friend.

Prior to this revelation, I had remembered being a well-known and powerful man who had conquered much of the world through brilliant strategy and brute force. I could recall scene after scene of gory conquering and death, but I could not recall his identity. It had also plagued me that in a drunken brawl and fight, he had killed his best general and closest friend.

Looking into Paul's eyes, I revisited the guilt, shame, horror and sorrow of my actions. They seemingly knew no bounds. It was only after many hours of inconsolable sobbing that I could ask for forgiveness from Paul and the others I had injured.

At first it challenged me sorely to find compassion for the vile acts I had perpetrated on countless "innocent victims." It seemed I deserved nothing but opprobrium, revilement and condemnation for such draconian acts.

However, in reviewing these scenes, I sensed that more was required of me than self-indulgent regret and self-judgment. I sought to understand Alexander's inner motivations. While his purest intentions were to spread culture and learning, his methods were far from peaceful. He not only was part of the mentality of the day, but was a wounded and insecure young man trying to conquer his own fears and prove his worth. His pain resonated within me and seemed as immense as the empire he had created. I could understand that need and while this did not excuse his actions, I found compassion for his human experience.

In accepting the Alexander part of me, I realized that all of us had done it all and played every role. I saw the victims and perpetrators mutually attracted to each other, each playing their own part to perfection. From this vantage point I saw no true victim or perpetrator in any situation, just equal souls playing roles. This recognition freed me from the guilt, but not from the responsibility of making amends for my actions. Without the guilt, however, I could forgive my mistakes, ignorance and lack of awareness. I softened into a gentle compassion for my imperfections and those of others. For the moment it all was okay.

After these memories had surfaced, I remembered dwelling between dimensions and making the choice to enter this life. Sitting in council with my Guides, we drew up a loose blueprint in preparation for my return to Earth.

I remembered being conceived. An explosive burst of light and a tractor beam connected my spirit with my parents, who were in love at the time. Our three energies united creating a brilliantly illuminated matrix that allowed me to begin the process of incarnating as their daughter. I felt my etheric energies being squeezed down a vortex, whose tremendous force sucked me through its funnel into matter as cells taking form within my mother's womb.

Cell by cell, I grew a body. Floating peacefully in amniotic fluid I could sense the many biochemical fluctuations that occurred. I was keenly aware of my mother's circadian rhythms and tonalities of light as night brightened into day and day folded back into night. I could sense my mother's emotions in her interactions with other people, most especially with my father. I could tell when she was happy or afraid.

When the time came to leave my warm, suspended home, I was not at all certain I was ready to go. I had grown quite comfortable in the security and love that my mother had provided me. Despite my hesitancy, the force and pressure of her contractions began. After momentarily digging in my heels in resistance, I realized that these contractions were the embodiment of something familiar to me. They were part of the forces of Nature, which was much greater than I. So, resistance to such a force, which had its own operative intelligence, was futile.

Being born was my first opportunity to gracefully accept what was occurring, but I was sorely challenged. Convinced by the power of the next contraction's squeeze, I surrendered to being born.

As I entered into the world, was insensitively plunked onto a cold metallic slab and could hear another baby screaming nearby, my instinctive reaction was, "Oh, no, not this again! Not another life on Earth! What have I done?" Overwhelmed by the enormity of my decision to return to Earth I was momentarily convinced I had made a catastrophic mistake.

Then I became aware of my mother's love beaming upon me while she was thinking, "Oh, I remember you! We will again be the best of friends!" Relieved to be with her, I relaxed and telepathically expressed back, "I'm so happy to be with you too." This initial interaction set the tone for our relationship and we were indeed the best of friends. Despite the many difficulties we faced and resolved over the years, we never wavered from our closeness as the ground state of being and fundamental truth of our connection.

Her waves of love suddenly shifted. Now, angry thoughts about my father coursed through her. He had become entangled in Columbus Day Parade traffic and was delayed by several hours. By the time he arrived at the hospital she was seething with resentment and fear. She turned to me once more and telepathically communicated, "You're my deepest love, my truest one. You don't let me down like he does. I love your father, he's my companion, but if I had to choose right now between the two of you, it would be you."

Her message both pained and delighted me. The absoluteness of her love provided comfort and security. But I recoiled at the comparison of her love for my father and me. I felt instantly burdened by the enormous responsibility I felt in the face of her devotion and need. I naively vowed to strive to be everything she needed me to be.

I could feel my father at a distance, stuck in traffic. He was lost in a wash of self-recrimination for not anticipating holiday congestion and seeking an alternate route. I could feel him reaching to me through his self-judgment, attempting to make contact. This event set the template for my relationship with my father as well, one of reaching for connection and almost making it, but not quite. My heart sank, "I've just arrived and this is a complicated mess already! I'm not sure I can handle all of this!"

When I was older, my mother and I often lounged on our family's floral print overstuffed chairs discussing our lives. Once I asked her, "What do you recall of my birth? Can you describe it to me in as great detail as possible?"

She replied without hesitation, "When I first laid eyes on you I was delighted and thought, 'Oh, I remember you! We will again be the best of friends!' There was another other baby crying in the room, and I was enraged by your father's delay." We were both amazed when my memories verified every detail of what she had experienced!

She was surprised that I had precise and accurate memories of a time that conventional wisdom believes was before an infant was capable of conscious memory. She went on to say that as I was growing up she never had to correct, instruct or explain anything to me. "The stove is hot, don't touch it," was not a necessary communication, as if my adult circuitry had already been wired. While growing up, I was eager to get childhood over with so that I could focus on the as of yet nameless thing I came here to do.

What was my mission and purpose? With no answer but a nagging feeling I had carried since birth, I engaged in self-reflection and self-examination. This practice was symptomatic of the same self-awareness that my dialogue with the Guides would eventually demand. From early on, knowing myself increasingly took on greater importance and meaning than the creature comforts of life. While I had an unnamable sense of who I was, I wanted to know why I was here.

To answer this question drove me to constantly seek from an inner burning need that called me onward. At each step, I had to voluntarily relinquish the comfort of the known to step off the cliff into the insecurity of the unknown. Incessantly challenged to release all that I held dear, I walked forward on sheer instinct and faith of necessity, only reluctantly relinquishing control.

Despite the fear of losing control, I persisted with my inner quest. But at each new step I needed some answers. At this point in my life, the only place to turn for that depth of contact was the Guides. With them I felt most at home as their words resonated with my own clearest inner voice. Despite persistent doubts and fears, I chose to follow that voice.

After the first reading, I had yearned incessantly for another encounter with the Guides. As the months went by, my impatience did not diminish and their absence was its own form of agony. It was almost a year before Paul came back to Boston.

At long last, the moment of my second reading arrived. Paul was in a different hotel than before, but followed the same ritual as the first time. He lit the candle, which sat on the little table next to the tape recorder, asked me to take off my shoes, stretch and sigh and chant seven ohms along with him.

This time I endured the ritual itself with more patience, but was holding my breath to see which spirits would come through.

As Paul slipped into trance and Spirit inhabited his body, I experienced feeling one with the energies again. This time a gentle voice with an Indian accent came to address me:

Greetings to you my dear friend, I am really happy to be able to come here. All of your existence is about learning the proper balance between personal mastery or self-empowerment and surrender. Most people have a very strong, compelling desire to go towards one or the other. It is not easy to understand where to put your creative energies and where to let go and surrender to the spiritual forces.

A sense of flow, or grace, is so important because it brings you the right things at the right time. Grace is very simple. It is dispensed, you might say, by that which is at the source of all existence. It is dispensed for one, and only one price, humility, or shall we say, gratitude, which will bring you a great peace of mind. It will allow you to let go of those things which are effortful and will allow grace to give them to you as a gift.

Another challenge along the path is when you are confronted by what appears to be fear. You might then seek to escape the challenge that fear represents. Instead, welcome your challenges, embrace them and meet them face to face. Remembering that you are not alone will help you resolve your fears.

I am Kira, your Master Guide, but not your Master Teacher. I am the one who has the easiest access to you right now. I serve as a key, like a master key to many locks. The time will come when I will no longer serve as that key, and another will have easier access. You will also become aware of your Master Teacher when the time is right.

He pierced me with a mysteriously significant look when he mentioned my Master Teacher, then lightened up again: *I must go so that others may speak with you. Is there one you would like me to draw in?*

My heart leapt as I asked to speak with the Chief so that I could bask in the warmth of that great love once again. Kira left abruptly after a gentle nod and suddenly I was with the Chief again.

I am Chief Great White Eagle. You are my friend, Anamika, and I consider myself privileged to include you among my associates. I am very happy to have this time with you through Paul. There's a subject we would like to discuss with you. Have you noticed what subject we have been avoiding?

I knew exactly what he was referring to. "Relationships," I blurted out.

Ahh, very perceptive. It is better to have relationships than to talk about them. If you want to talk about relationships, I'll talk. But there is something I want to ask you first. Are you happy?

"No, I can't say that I am. I still have a desperate longing inside, a burning desire for love."

Happiness really has to do with learning how to be satisfied in the knowledge that you are doing what feels right for you. It also has to do with not trying to push away sadness, upset, or conflict, hmmh? You are helping other people integrate all of their experiences because that is also a part of what you are here to do. You must simply allow yourself all of your feelings, not only your joys, but all of your challenges and pain. In accepting your feelings you can attain a high level of serenity and happiness in life.

The time will come, Anamika, when all of these challenges about relationships will end. They finish when the inner fighting stops. You know the fight is not with the universe, it is really a fight with your own way of looking at things. You can't win that fight. You are equal to the opponent, and the opponent is equal to you. Since everything is you, you do not win by fighting, but by allowing.

Your power handles things with so much more energy when there's less fighting going on inside. Watch, you will see this happen today and for the rest of your days so long as you remember this. We will lend you our energy. Let your spirit become one with the power of our spirit. Then, go about your business realizing that this same power that moved through you will move other matters. This is a lesson in mastery. If you are willing to let Spirit come through you, then we can all come to you, with you directing the power and the power directing you. It will be back and forth. Then, the Great Intelligence that is far beyond that which you individually access will be yours to share. I must go now.

And with that he was gone, leaving me nearly breathless from the interaction. Another Guide entered Paul's body, changing his face to that of a very young, almost angelic presence with a high feminine voice.

Guess who I am?

"An angel?" I guessed.

No, but you're very close. I'm a seraph. We express a little bit differently than angels. My name is Constance. Right now you are having a lot of life lessons in how to be really happy. You can expect to find yourself happier and happier by being with yourself. I don't mean being alone. You're going to start to experience more and more pleasure in the moments that come to you as you are with yourself. Life can get wonderful when you are with yourself consciously. That's where all the beauty is. In touch with your own energy, you start to glow and that glow is what draws the partner to you. It also draws us to you and other miracles as well.

You're going to have lots of experiences in glowing, and I know all about that since I glow a lot. I want to work with you to help that radiance shine ever more brightly. I also have a suggestion. Develop a closer rapport with God now. Know God more intimately, like your dearest friend. God wants to be that intimate with you.

"Constance," I interrupted in exasperation, "I don't even know who or what God is. I don't even believe in God. What is God?"

I can't tell you because you can only know by being in love with it. God is that which inspires a devotional ecstasy that is decidedly personal rather than impersonal. God is like an incredible artist with a temperament and motivations very different than you might conceptualize. The Creator, the Source definitely has its own distinct flair and flavor. Each being experiences a Creator with a unique personality custom designed for that being; not because they need it but because it's like a lover. That's romantic, you see. God is like an intimate lover and the universe is one big romance.

"How do you know that's going to happen for me?" I was stunned by her words.

Well, maybe you don't understand what I am. I'm a herald. The Source sends me and those like me to help people get ready to know God.

"So what I need to do now is to develop my own personal and intimate relationship with a God I don't know?" I asked incredulously.

Yes, you've got it! She sounded genuinely excited, like a little child.

I didn't know what on earth she was talking about. I meant it when I said I didn't believe in God. I was raised a reformed Jew and many of the members of our synagogue did not believe in God. We were Jews by tradition, but not by religion. Our "religion" was a cultural and political statement by an oppressed people who were determined to be liberated and sustain their homeland. We had been brought up to believe that people needed to depend on their rational abilities to create the sort of life that produced happiness. We believed that life after death was not possible; all we had was here and now. The intangible did not exist.

Regularly, we scoffed at those who practiced religious beliefs. Regular attendance at Temple was viewed as superstitious nonsense that was beneath us. As we listened to our religious churchgoing neighbors pay homage to their God, a gray-haired man in the sky, and to Jesus who was their savior, we would roll our eyes as if saying, "What ignorance! How could they believe this nonsense?" We were an intellectual group concerned with empowering ourselves and with not using religion as a crutch.

We had a strength of will and an enormity of pride that was born of our ability to survive. "We survived the holocaust! We survived the pogroms, we survived millennia of persecution and now it's up to us. We can't sit idly and wait for others to insure our freedom. We must take charge of our own lives and make sure we are never persecuted again."

This perspective was the food of my early years. In stark contrast, now I had this seraph telling me I needed to have a more intimate relationship with God. Needless to say, I was appalled and repulsed. The idea seemed vile and despicably weak. Nevertheless, inexplicably I found myself opening to her suggestions. For some reason, I decided to act on faith and to risk trusting that there was a God who wanted an intimate relationship with me, as long as I didn't have to really believe it!

I could sense that my need to aggressively and powerfully control my affairs was really a desperate effort to protect myself and to find security. What I had vaingloriously described as controlling my destiny only showed that I actually felt overwhelmed and powerless. My atheistic beliefs had contributed to the feelings of isolation and alienation that had tormented my childhood. I had both sensed and denied that there was more to life than our rational, material world and I had lived with this contradiction within me.

I had been denying the very thing I had been connected to since childhood, the glorious realms beyond the tangible and visible. In these dimensions of reality was the profound harmony and serenity that I found in dialogue with the Guides.

I was able to shed my rational, analytical beliefs because of the relationship that I had had with Nature throughout my childhood. Nature's gentle comforting presence had prepared me to accept the dialogue with the Guides as a more intense, articulate form of itself. To me, Nature was not yet God. I still regarded it simply as a part of material reality. Therefore, it wasn't that great a stretch to accept the Guides without addressing the greater theological and existential questions regarding the existence of God.

I still comfortably drew a distinction between Spirit Guides and God. I needed the Guides as an intermediate, transitional consciousness because I could only face the vulnerability inherent in relinquishing control and opening to the potential of my spirit a little at a time.

How could I build a relationship with a God I did not know? Almost immediately I was confronted with a situation in which to put Constance's instructions into practice. I discovered I was pregnant! This news came as an unexpected shock for two reasons. Firstly, I had just ended my relationship with this man and emphatically did not want him, a child with him or a child with anyone else. Secondly, I had been told at eighteen that I had a slight hormonal imbalance and would never become pregnant.

I immediately set an appointment for an abortion but was horrified at the prospect. I didn't object on moral grounds, rather the thought of it stimulated distant memories of physical violation such as rape and mutilation. My hope was to miscarry rather than abort.

Alighting upon what I thought was a clever idea, I decided that if God wanted to have a relationship with me, God could do something to prove it. "Okay, Source," I demanded defiantly, "if you want an intimate relationship with me, here's what I want you to do. As I need a concrete sign that you exist, here's the deal. I need a miscarriage on August 31st!"

Having issued this ultimatum, I had only ten days to experience pregnancy. Realizing this, I allowed myself to bask in the soft, rosy aura pregnant women exude. I was surprised to find a great desire to commune with the spirit of the baby growing within me, for initially I had wanted to put this whole episode behind me as quickly as possible. Just as I had done as a fetus inside my own mother, I was able to communicate telepathically with the spirit of the baby, but this time from a mother's perspective. We fell deeply in love, rendering the ten days bittersweet with the knowledge that the connection in this form would soon end.

Several days before the scheduled abortion, I sensed the spirit withdrawing. The gentle communication stopped. In its place was a void, a melancholy emptiness. This quickly dissolved into pain, a stark contrast to the delicious warmth in which I had been steeped with the spirit.

As the day of reckoning drew closer, I began to doubt what little faith I had placed in God. Plunging headlong into despair, I was certain that I had been a complete fool to set up a ridiculous test only to prove to myself that there was no God.

August 31st arrived. No blood. As the day wore on, I became increasingly frantic. Would I miscarry, or not? Would I need the abortion I had scheduled? Evening arrived and still there was no release. I collapsed in tears of despair on the cold tile of the bathroom floor. Shaking my fist at the heavens I screamed, "You see, I knew it, there is no God!" Then suddenly, with no warning, there was a torrent of blood flowing as if someone had heard my tortured prayer and opened the valve. Needless to say, I was as shocked as I had been when I found out I was pregnant!

Collecting myself, I got up from the cold tile and lay down gently on my bed to rest. The cramping had begun. I drifted in and out of sleep as the contractions of the miscarriage continued throughout the night. When the first light of morning broke, I drove to the doctor to be examined. She confirmed that I was indeed miscarrying, but was in no danger.

Simultaneously overwhelmed with grief, loss and gratitude, I sensed the Guides gently comforting me. Between tears they showed me a vision of the baby's spirit now surrounded and held by other spirits. They informed me that the spirit had never had an intention of being born, but had desired practice crossing between the worlds. They disclosed that they hadn't shared this information before because I needed to act on faith. I had to accept the rightness of what was occurring without knowing the outcome in advance.

After this experience I felt a deeper connection with Source than ever before. I began to understand that my every day experiences were my spiritual path. The spiritual path was not outside of me. It was living the principles that resonated as truth on a daily basis.

The pregnancy experience was my first real test of this new perspective and it was a mighty one indeed as I was dealing with life and death. As the results turned out positively, my trust in the existence of God increased. I now felt ready to commit myself to going the distance. I was prepared to continue on faith that God existed and to challenge remaining feelings of separation and fear. I became increasingly interested in discovering more about what Constance meant about building an intimate relationship with "My Beloved."

CHAPTER 3

Shamuki

The entire universe and all of God is your true lover.
You cannot find the love you are looking for
through another person alone. – Philos

My newfound trust birthed a considerably stronger flow of energy as I worked with my clients. My healing capabilities were enhanced and I was able to effect far more profound interventions as I allowed the divine energy to flow through me.

I realized that I was evolving beyond atheism and strict rationality. In this evolution of faith, doubt played a prominent role. Despite the constant experience of Source in my life, I wasn't able to simply accept this new paradigm without fear and doubt. It was all too new and nagging reservations persisted. I had to constantly remind myself that the glorious feelings of rightness that pervaded my life were the validation of my deepening faith. Even though I couldn't prove it, I knew in the core of my being that what was occurring was wonderful; the energy was real. Day after day I practiced standing in the truth that this energy was Spirit. Spirit seemed to hold and support me through these serious doubts. The transformation of doubt into certainty was part of the process and it would take time.

The more I opened to the energies coursing through me, the more I trusted them. I couldn't comfortably yet call them God, so I called them Spirit or the Energies much in the way I called this force Nature as a child. I was learning to trust that the Energies or Spirit would always come and do the work. I didn't have to do it all myself.

As I relaxed the fearful survival clench in my belly, I attuned to those energies, allowing them to flow strongly and guide me. It became quite evident that they were stronger and wiser than I was. Without Spirit, I was a limited finite personality. When blended with Spirit I was elevated to my limitless, infinite self.

Despite my doubts and fears, I relied on the Energies. Healing occurred in my clients time after time. Gaining confidence, I risked letting go even more into an increasingly potent flow. Some of my clients were quite skeptical. Their skepticism gave voice to my own doubts, which I had to answer with clarity and confidence. Ironically, their doubts served to strengthen my certainty that the Energies were real and reliable.

Soon people began flocking to my door. It was becoming more difficult to deny that something significant was happening. My clients' progress far exceeded anything I had achieved with a more conventional approach. Visible signs of their joy and well-being I could no longer deny, as they were ending stale relationships, finding more fulfilling love, resolving inner conflicts, embarking on new careers and improving their health. They were living proof that something magical was afoot.

Simultaneously, I was suffering severe health problems. While my clients were improving dramatically, I was degenerating. Zealous in my efforts to help as many people as possible, I worked sixteen-hour days, seven days a week. Through overwork I found myself flattened with six viruses and bottomless fatigue. By sheer force of will I continued to work through constant fevers, aches, chills and stabbing sore throats. So possessed was I by my mission of getting "there," it never occurred to me to stop and see where "there" was, or if indeed there was any "there" at all.

In the midst of one of these viral bouts, a heavy, middle-aged woman came for a healing. She complained of a chronic stomach pain of unknown origins. Extensive medical tests had revealed nothing. As I scanned her energy field, what I saw was a large gelatinous blob of green slime in her abdomen. When I asked if she was aware of its presence, she said that all she could sense was the pain and didn't have a clue as to why it was there.

As I looked more carefully, I saw that this blob had a round squat body and a recognizable face with distinct features, like a ghoulish demon. He was spewing green slime, sticking out his tongue, and threatening to grab me around the neck if I tried to dislodge him from his comfortable lair.

Resorting to a tactic I had read in a healing book, I retorted, "I'm not scared of you!" Actually, that wasn't true. I was terrified, but determined to stand my ground. He had to go. I focused a beam of energy into the woman's abdomen, surrounded the demon, reached my etheric hand into her body and began to pull. He resisted, redoubled his efforts to maintain his entrenched position. Before I knew it, we were engaged in a deadly fight for which I did not have the strength in my weakened state. By sheer force of will, I managed to extract his protesting form from my client. He glared at me threateningly as I pulled him out of the woman. Jumping out of my grasp, he flattened himself against the ceiling in the farthest corner of my healing room, sulking and glowering at me.

With an explosion of delight the woman proclaimed that the pain was entirely gone and this was the best she had felt in ten years. She could hardly contain her euphoria as I escorted her out of the house.

I, on the other hand, was exhausted and drained. I had been tired before this episode and was now stretched well beyond my limits. I returned to the healing room to clear the demon from my house. This involved an effort to project energy into him thereby raising his vibration and sending him into the light. In my depleted state, this normally simple procedure was beyond my capacity.

In resignation, I left the room, closing the door tightly in hopes of containing him until I had more energy. Seeking to restore myself I went into the kitchen for vitamins. No sooner had I taken a swig of water to swallow the pills than the demon appeared, grabbed me around the neck choking me so hard that the pills became lodged in my throat. I couldn't draw a breath and was certain I was going to die. Gasping for air, I fell to the floor. The impact of hitting the hard tiled floor dislodged the pills and the demon. Mercifully, I could breathe once again. The demon laughed hideously and disappeared back into the healing room.

Instantly I left the house to spend the night with Gabriella and regain some strength. I prayed he would not follow me to her house. Fortunately, he didn't and I spent the night in peace. The next day I asked several friends to help clear him from my house. Together, our joint energy raised the vibration sufficiently to escort him into another dimension with ease. He turned into light and disappeared.

Later that day he appeared for a brief moment in an entirely different state of being. He was luminous and gave me a very gentle, benign smile. To my utter shock, he apologized for playing out his former hideous consciousness on me, and thanked me for liberating him from it. I forgave him and smiled back. While greatly relieved, that battle left an indelible impression on me. As the gentle voice had so wisely advised before I entered this life, you don't win by fighting.

After this incident I redoubled my efforts to allow, not to fight, and returned to work humbled. I noticed that this gentler attitude allowed yet a greater flow of energy once again and my practice became more effective and popular than ever. So much so, that people began asking me not only for personal healing but to teach what I was practicing. They hungered for instruction in working with energy for healing, accessing Spirit Guides and understanding the principles of awakening. It seemed that no sooner had I learned something new than a group gathered to learn.

Shamuki was accompanying me through all of this new growth. He assisted in the healing sessions and classes. Oh, I haven't mentioned Shamuki, my beautiful Golden Retriever. His story actually began long before he came to me.

Shamuki was the culmination of a close journey I had had with dogs. Since childhood, Golden Retrievers had been an integral part of my family. My mother treated our first Retriever, Juggins, as the sixth child. He was my intimate playmate and constant companion. Juggins would come to school with us each day and wait outside until the final bell rang. Even though this was against the school's rules, somehow in his case it was allowed. If I had to stay too late after school, he would take the bus home by himself, sitting up proudly in the seat. The driver would let him off at the appropriate stop and he would run the mile from the bus stop home. He even attended a year of college with me, living in my dorm room. His college career ended abruptly when he was reprimanded for barking in the library of all places! I had to send him home.

Living without a dog was an adjustment. After college, I invited Kairo, a rambunctious Golden Retriever pup to come and live with me. Kairo and I were together for about a year when one week, a series of very strange events which seemed like signs occurred. First, he lost his favorite bandana, then almost got hit by a car. Next, I found myself turning over the cushions of the couch on which he had taken up residence. I had never flipped over these cushions to the clean side during that entire year. Lastly, I found myself pulling up weeds in my front yard, which I had never done before. Kairo was inspecting the area and rolling in the grass. I had never allowed Kairo in the front yard off leash because the house fronted on the street. For some unknown reason, there we were. As I was yanking these weeds out by the roots, Kairo suddenly bolted into the street and was hit by a truck right before my eyes. In shock and hysteria I ran to him to find that his back was broken and he was bleeding profusely. I was sobbing hysterically as he looked me calmly right in the eyes, wagged his tail weakly and telepathically communicated, "I love you and it's okay."

Frantically bundling him into the car, we rushed to the vet. In the car I was out of my mind screaming, "Don't die! Don't die!" Suddenly realizing how selfish, not to mention pointless that sentiment was, I had to give him permission to leave. Taking a deep breath I consented, "It's okay if you go, Kairo. Do what's best for you." No sooner were the words out of my mouth than Kairo left his body. I felt his spirit rise up and explode into light. We never even made it to the vet. I returned home in a daze of loss, grief and shock.

Many of my students at that time were devotees of Swami Chidvilasananda. I had never been interested in Gurus, but when I got back home, there was a living vision of this Guru in my living room. She began singing the old song, "There's a hole in your bucket dear Liza, dear Liza." She was accurately poking at the troublesome and omnipresent hole in my soul. Kairo's absence made that hole even more poignant. She said that Kairo's journey was to show me the emptiness in my soul. I knew I needed to let myself feel that void, grieve it and accept it. It meant I had to stop frantically running around looking for answers and instead discover what lay underneath my desperate search for the One.

As I began to explore the underpinnings of my psyche, I sensed the spirit of another Golden Retriever. He contacted me with the intention of coming to live with me when the time was right. Soon, I felt that he had come into this world, so I began to look all over the state of Massachusetts for him. I interviewed fifty adorable puppies and each was precious, but not my dog. Coming up empty handed I began to doubt that I had heard the message clearly. Perhaps he wasn't here yet. With these thoughts, I let go of the search.

One day a breeder called me with news, "I hear you're looking for a male Retriever. We have one male, the pick of the litter. He is exceptionally beautiful and we were going to keep him, but for some reason my wife has decided that this puppy is not for us. Do you want to have a look at him?" My immediate reaction was to say no. I didn't want further disappointment. Fifty times was enough. However, a small voice within, which I couldn't deny, urged me to consent.

At the breeder's home, there were eight adorable, fuzzy little puppies. The seven females were squealing and squiggling on top of each other as they played. In the corner, all by himself was the one male. Unnecessarily, the breeder pointed and said, "That's the male. He keeps to himself and responds to no one. He's very healthy and exceptionally handsome but barely eats.

As I doubtfully approached the enclosure, the male puppy jumped up and bounded toward me. The breeder opened the gate allowing the pup to continue unabated toward me. I scooped him up and gently squeezed him to me. The breeder's jaw dropped open as the puppy joyfully began licking my nose and silently exclaiming, "I found you, I finally found you! I've been waiting! Here you are at last!" I responded with equal joy and amazement,

"It has taken so long, but here you are!" I was still savoring the delicious scent of puppy breath on my nose.

We fell in love instantly. Holding him tightly, I turned to the breeder saying definitively, "This is my dog." "I guess it is!" was his reply. "You're the only person that pup has responded to!"

Floating on a cloud, I carried him out to the car and positioned him carefully in my lap for the hour long drive home. He promptly confirmed his puppyhood by throwing up all over my clothes. Laughing, I teased him, "This is our initiation, puppy style," and we proceeded home. From that moment on, each time I looked into his eyes I experienced the deepest love I had ever known.

It took me a month to find his name. Every day I repeated the question, "What is your name?" I heard only fragments that seemed to fit partially but didn't yet make sense. I heard "Shami" and "Kabuki." Asking for clarification, I received, *'Sha' is the heart sound, meaning of the heart or love. 'Ki' is 'chi' or energy."* "Love energy?" I asked. It still didn't fit. Then one day, while playing with the words, I combined them. "Shamuki. Is that it?" I asked him.

"Yes!" he responded, "that's it! *Sha* is of the heart, *mu* is the universe and *ki* is energy. My name is Shamuki, which means love is the universal energy. That's who I am. I am an aspect of Yeshua in dog form. I am your psychic guardian, teacher and protector. I am your familiar, your animal companion as in the days of old. Kairo left to pave the way for me because I am your true companion."

I was elated. What an immensely loving spirit with a unique and wonderful name, I mused. Anamika and Shamuki. Anamika and Shamuki. It was a mouthful, but somehow it fit! Shamuki was the living embodiment of the great love I was seeking. He loved passionately, unabashedly and absolutely in a way I had never experienced. A true master, he radiated pure, unequivocal joy. Every day, I prayed to be more like him.

Sometimes I doubted my objectivity about his qualities because he was my dog and I was in love with him. However, my doubts were put to rest as person after person who encountered him came away with the same experience I had. People stopped me in the street to speak with him every time we went out. Those who knew him called him, "God in a fur coat," or "Master Shamuki." I was in awe of his healing abilities as well as his compassion. People sent thank you letters to the house addressed to Shamuki. When they entered the house, it was "Hello Shamuki!" As an afterthought, out of politeness they would add, "Oh, yes, hello to you too, Anamika."

Shamuki participated in all of the healing sessions. Sometimes he quietly assisted by holding the person in his energy from across the room. At other times he would play an active part. One client, who was describing her desolate early life, lapsed into despair as she expressed her certainty that she would never experience connectedness. Shamuki, who had been lying silently by my side, arose and gently approached her. He placed one paw on her heart and smothered her with tender kisses. She burst into tears of relief and gratitude exclaiming that she had never felt so loved before.

On another occasion, a woman was grieving the loss of her beloved Afghan Hound. Shamuki invited the spirit of her dog into his body. Suddenly, she bent over to smell him exclaiming, "My dog had a very distinctive smell. That exact smell is present now in Shamuki! Then, she looked into Shamuki's eyes and saw the eyes of her dog. Tears streamed down her face. What a beautiful reunion they shared through Shamuki! I could see that Shamuki's eyes had taken on a different shape and expression. I was reminded of how Paul's face and aura changed as he channeled different Guides. Through this experience I became aware that Shamuki had a gift of channeling, which from then on I witnessed frequently.

Often, if I wasn't feeling well and couldn't go on I would say, "Shamuki, I have a sore throat and have one more client to go. Can you help me?" He would put his paw on my throat or just send a beam of energy there and the pain would lift instantly. Such was Shamuki's way. My female clients formed a Shamuki fan club and agreed that if they could ever find a man like Shamuki they would grab him in an instant.

One day, Shamuki and I went for our usual morning walk in the field across from our house. While he was romping in his joyous fashion, instead of keeping pace with him I stopped to eat an apple and to watch him. I began to notice the sun's gentle warmth on the side of my neck, as if fingers were caressing me. My senses suddenly awoke, as if I had been completely asleep until that moment. I could truly *feel* as if for the first time. The sun's fingers were pouring energy through my skin, filling each cell, enlivening my body. The Earth was reaching up her hands, holding my feet. I could feel the very fabric of the universe celebrating its *Isness,* its beingness. I could feel the Source in its unmanifest potential and in its creation.

The distinct voice of one of the Guides spoke inside of me as clearly as if he were standing directly before me. The voice, which I later came to identify as Philos, was deep, resonant and philosophical. *The entire universe and all of*

38-Into the Heart of the Beloved

God is your true lover. You cannot find the love you are looking for through another person alone. In that moment I felt ecstatically merged with all aspects of nature, as I were a part of an ever-changing kaleidoscope of life.

The states of being I touched through allowing, trust and surrender far surpassed everything I had ever achieve through force of will. If this is really what life is about, it's beautiful I announced to the sun. "I choose to continue to surrender!" I declared to all of creation.

Shortly after that experience, I took a trip to the mountains near Santa Cruz, California, overlooking the Pacific Ocean for a week-long retreat. My intention for this silent retreat was to follow my inner voice without reservation, trusting that wherever it led would be the highest place to go. By now I was in the habit of listening inwardly for messages, but I had never attempted to listen every minute of every day for an entire week.

This degree of consistent focus was a formidable task in concentration and deep listening. All twenty of us at the retreat, although aware of each other, were primarily focused inwardly. My inner world consisted of my breath, sound, emotion, body movements and changes of sensations, thoughts and feelings.

The exquisite beauty of the natural setting supported our inner journey. We were located on a mountaintop surrounded by statuesque redwoods. Dense fog rolled in over the mountains in the early morning, only to be burned away by the sun revealing a sparkling ocean clearly visible at a distance. Inquisitive but shy deer, an ancient white horse and a few scruffy stray dogs completed the scene.

The first day was torturous and seemed to go on forever. Gradually, as I became acclimated to attending to every nuance of my inner flow, time ceased. In this timeless place the days and nights blended into one unbroken stream of life. It was on one of those days that my life force broke through in a way that irrevocably changed my life.

I awoke to the feeling of rain. The air was heavy and the sky threatening. I asked inwardly how to begin the day. Spirit directed me to get up, put on sneakers and warm clothing and go out to walk on the mountain. I followed a path that beckoned and soon found myself at the foot of an extremely steep incline.

The Guides were propelling me on at a good clip and wanted me to continue up the steep hill at that pace. I knew I was not physically capable of this task and asked Spirit to infuse me with enough energy to carry me up the hill. Inhaling deeply, I began.

The incline was horrendous and after an embarrassingly short distance my thigh muscles burned, my lungs ached, and I gasped for breath. Images flashed before me of dying on a pyre from smoke inhalation, being sent to death in a gas chamber and drowning at sea. Somehow, through all of this, I made it to the top. Exhausted, I crawled back to the large retreat room and lay down on my mat to rest. Within several minutes, the inner voice instructed me to get up and do the same climb again.

By now my breath had stabilized and my leg muscles had sufficiently relaxed, so while the thought wasn't pleasant, I didn't put up too much resistance. The second climb went much like the first except that it seemed I was building some stamina. Even though I was still gasping for air, my legs seemed to have a bit more strength.

Back in the lodge I collapsed again and rested. The second climb had taken more from me than I had realized. As I was drifting in a dreamy state, I could hear thunder in the background and sensed the air becoming even more dense. I heard the Guides say, "Get on your sneakers. It's time to go out again." I couldn't believe what I was hearing! I had already pushed beyond my limits twice, and now it had even begun to drizzle. The first two times I had followed the instructions without question. This time I balked. "What if it starts to rain hard? What if I get wet? What if I can't manage to complete the climb?" A firm voice responded, "Put on your sneakers. It's time to go. NOW!" Reluctantly, I complied, remembering my commitment to listen for and follow my inner guidance absolutely.

Putting on a heavy sweatshirt and sneakers, I set out for the third time. By now it was drizzling steadily and I hoped the heavy rain would hold off until I returned. As fate would have it, as soon as I reached the base of the steep incline, the skies opened up. Thunder crashed, escorting a torrential downpour. I was soaked to the bone within seconds. Puffing and panting up the impossibly steep and now slippery incline, I felt like I was about to die. My sneakers grew heavier as they became waterlogged and the thick muddy clay was clinging to the sides of the shoes making each step more impossible than the last. In utter exasperation I shook my fist at the heavens, "What are you guys doing to me? What's going on around here anyway?"

Soon there was no energy left for thought. I was forced to surrender to the movement, the rain, the steep incline, the cold air searing my lungs and the burning muscles in my legs. Slipping out of ordinary consciousness, I was pulled into an altered state as if some higher force had taken control of my body and was now carrying me effortlessly up the hill.

40-Into the Heart of the Beloved

After reaching the top, the force left me and I staggered back to my room. I stripped off the drenched clothing and put on something warm and dry as quickly as I could. Exhausted beyond belief, I plunked down onto the edge of a hard wooden bunk bed. In utter frustration and incomprehension, I demanded of the heavens, "Okay, guys, why the torture?"

The response came in a wave of energy that almost knocked me over backwards, then pushed me forward again.Then, again I was rocked back and forth so forcefully that I could feel my sitz bones boring into the wooden bed frame. The rocking persisted, picking up speed and shifted from very large movements to increasing smoother and more refined sensations.

I began to feel a powerful hot current of pleasurable fire making its way up my spine. It felt like a serpent had uncoiled in the base of my spine and was forcefully pushing its way upward. As it did, my body began to buzz and shake involuntarily. Tears welled up and sobs emerged from somewhere deep within.

I rocked, sobbed and shook uncontrollably as this serpent of fire wound its way up my spine, burning out the debris in its path. By the time the snake reached my head the tears and shaking had subsided. They were replaced by an ecstatic flow, which enlivened every cell. My entire body was now vibrating with a new energy.

As the current pierced the top of my head I became aware of another movement beginning in the sacrum, as if two smaller snakes were waking up. This time, instead of the one current flowing up the center, there were three currents, one on each side of the center, weaving back and forth across the central one It slowly dawned on me that these three currents were the kundalini snakes I had read of in Indian literature.

I remembered hearing stories of people going insane from a premature kundalini release, as the energy is extremely potent. Despite my fear of being harmed, I was in ecstasy. The wisdom of the Guides' strategy, which had previously seemed like madness to me, suddenly became clear. They had pushed my body so hard that it opened up beyond its usual resistance so that the energy could break through.

As the central current or snake and the two side snakes completed their upward journey, they stayed present, creating a smooth golden flow. As they pierced the crown of my head, wave after wave of ecstasy washed over me like an eternal waterfall. I was in heaven! I luxuriated in these energies for hours, absorbing well-deserved healing balm for my aching body. Ever since, whenever I focus on these snakes, they rise up, spill over and wash me clean.

CHAPTER 4

SAKKARA TEMPLE OF HEALING

Awakening or ascension is the
discovery of who and what you really are.
The truth is that each person is a self-contained divine
entity that is continually exuding and receiving vibration
from the Creator, the Source, the All That Is. - Sun Bear

Eager to discuss my recent experiences with the Guides, I called Paul to find out when he would next be in Boston. He wasn't sure, but to my delight, informed me that he did readings over the phone. This good news meant that I could speak with the Guides regularly. I had the sense they were preparing me for something, but I did not know what. When I spoke with them, they kept mentioning the highest path, warning that the highest pathway could be as wrenching and debilitating as the lowest if I were not properly prepared.

They went on to tell me that the highest path often means facing more than what you thought you could handle. They said I would be given opportunities that might seem daunting, but that I should not let that dissuade me. Finally, they said, timing is of great importance, and what is crucial is one's own sense of when change is right.

I couldn't imagine what kind of change they were intimating. My mind imagined various kinds of losses: I'd be out on the street, I'd lose all of my money and I'd be robbed of my material comforts. I'd become an ascetic with little to eat, I'd live in a monastery and wear robes, or I would sleep on dirt floors. Rationally, I knew that this was not what they meant, but I had no control of my mind's fearful imaginings. At the same time, I was excited about unknown possibilities and potential. Something was stirring and I was eager for it to be revealed.

By now, I had been in private practice as a psychotherapist and later as an energy healer for over fifteen years. As the Guides had so accurately forecasted, I began to sense a powerful change approaching which would change the nature of my work. There was an urgency, an immediacy about the change, so I suspected that the new form would be arriving soon.

The first whispers of this change came as I was working with a client who had a brain tumor. Initially, he wanted me to "fix" his tumor. I explained that his healing might take him into life or into death and that that wasn't up to me. He was the uncle of my lover Isaac and reminded me of my father in several ways. They were about the same age and stature. Both possessed a kind and gentle heart, but did not express their feelings easily. They both had little emotional involvement with their families. My father had kept his distance through his work, while Isaac's uncle had spent his time at the golf course and polishing his Mercedes. They were both somewhat alienated from their wives and children.

My father's emotional reticence was painful to me as a child. Although he was generous with his money and other physical resource, his lack of demonstrable affection precluded forming a close emotional bond with him and I had always resented this. Therefore, I was surprised that I felt compassion toward Isaac's uncle. Somehow, I found no need to project the anger I felt toward my father onto him. Instead, I was empathetic to his plight. He was in a great deal of emotional as well as physical pain and was now willing to make some changes in his life. My desire was to help him do so.

I reminded him that it's never too late to open to greater love. Even one moment of authentic love shared with his wife and sons was worth everything and that he didn't have to wait. Reassured, he began to relax and open, feeling understood and forgiven. As he forgave himself for his past, thus dissolving his self-judgment, I forgave my father. Isaac's uncle and I had surrendered into a beautiful love together, each healing something significant in our own heart.

As my soul filled with peace, I became aware that a strong presence had joined us. I felt myself drawn into its embrace and consumed by its power. Suddenly, it spoke aloud within me, as if a radio had turned on in my head. *Shaqqara, Saqqara, Sakkara, Temple of Healing. In Thy Presence Be I Whole.*

I was startled by the strength and clarity of the voice, not to mention the content. Instantly realizing that this moment was not to be lost, I excused myself from Isaac's uncle to write down the message. Listening to the whispers of light again, I received an explanation. *Saqqara is the ancient Egyptian temple of sound and healing used for the process of awakening. The 'sh' is the pre-Egyptian pronunciation. You will use it as Sakkara because the 'k' resonates with Anamika.*

"Use what?" I asked in confusion. This time there was only silence.

I was overcome by the beauty of this experience, but failed to comprehend its meaning. I looked down in amazement at the words I had written: *Sakkara Temple of Healing, In Thy Presence Be I Whole*. Still in a daze, I wondered what this could possibly mean. All that I could understand was that it seemed to fit the pattern of the opportunities of the highest path the Guides had forecast. While I was quite willing to take advantage of new opportunities, I didn't comprehend what the opportunity was.

Impatient as ever, I wanted to understand the meaning of Sakkara immediately. Finding that this wasn't possible, I reluctantly returned to Isaac's uncle. While I had been across the room writing down the message about Sakkara, he had come to the realization that his life needed to change. He resolved to put love first in his life and ask for forgiveness from his wife and sons.

As if in answer to the need for my life to change as well, the next day I received a brochure in the mail. "Come tour Egypt, the ancient Nile and the Temple of sound and healing at Saqqara." I was amazed at the synchronicity, but now even more confused as to its meaning. Although the brochure seemed to be an attempt to further illuminate me, I still had no idea what some ancient Egyptian temple had to do with my "highest path." However, I felt compelled to follow the clues as they presented like a magical mystery tour. Sakkara was calling and I needed to follow and discover its meaning. Even though I did not yet know what Sakkara was it seemed vital to my life at this juncture. Thus, my next task was to find out what it was.

To embark upon this new journey of discovery, it seemed that I had to give up my entire practice. Although very frightened about letting go of my clients, I began preparing them for the change. I informed them that I would no longer be available for private sessions as I was heading in a new direction that I could not yet articulate. Not surprisingly, many people felt I was being impulsive and following a fantasy. Others warned that I was not making a sound financial decision.

I had to agree that leaving my practice did not appear to be wise, but the feeling of Sakkara was so absolute that I had no choice but to take the risk. I had to follow this inner voice. Taking a deep breath, I approached the edge of the proverbial cliff and jumped. I let go of my entire work life as I had known it in a period of three short weeks.

After terminating with my clients, I gathered a group of twelve of my most sensitive students of energy healing to participate in my inquiry into Sakkara. As soon as we were comfortably seated in a circle, an expectant hush fell over the room. I invited Sakkara to make its presence known, not sure that anything would happen.

Suddenly, powerful healing energies began to rain down upon us. First, a large etheric step pyramid descended into the room in the exact shape of the step pyramid in Egypt. Then a sphere appeared, representing the space-time continuum in which we live. Within the sphere was a three-dimensional star tetrahedron, the Star of David, symbolizing union with the divine and the principles, "As above, so below, as within so without."

A crystalline column descended into the center of the room and within it twelve golden strands of DNA were spiraling. These strands radiated out from the crystalline column and connected with each person's DNA. Following the column, a cube, a rectangle, a golden mean spiral and many other geometric forms appeared.

A large, rapidly spinning vortex strategically placed itself in the center of the circle. As it accelerated or decelerated as needed, it transmuted the low frequency energies of fear into white light. A golden column connected down through each person's crown as multicolored sheets of energy permeated the room.

Golden strands of light wrapped around the outside of the group and through each person's heart, weaving us together into one unified organism as an infinity sign appeared in the center of the room, intersecting the crystalline column. Then, a multitude of infinity signs drew together giving the appearance of many gyroscopes oscillating rapidly.

After the geometric forms appeared, the door, which had been tightly latched, dramatically blew open and a powerful gust of cool wind entered the room. Standing in the center for all to behold was the etheric form of Yeshua along with angels, Ascended Masters and Archangels. Yeshua walked around the room touching each person on the heart. I noticed each person look at him as if he was visible and many burst into tears as they felt his sweet compassion.

Several of the Ascended Masters surrounded each of us. The Masters would circulate throughout the room approaching whoever was in need of healing. Shamuki also made the rounds, placing his paw on a heart, laying his head in a lap, or licking a tearful face. By now, the room was pulsing with such a charge of energy that people were experiencing spontaneous physical movement, emotional expression, insight, revelation and awakening.

Stunned at the power and beauty of what was occurring, I knew that something extraordinary had happened and that the course of my life had just irrevocably changed. Was Sakkara the answer to one of my two questions, what is my mission? Even though this was all brand new, in an instant I was certain. I knew that invoking and transmitting these stunningly powerful energies of healing and awakening called Sakkara, which were given to me as a gift, was indeed my purpose, my mission and my service to humanity.

Overwhelmed by this first experience of Sakkara, I called Paul for a reading in hopes that the Guides could explain the extraordinary events that had just occurred. Sun Bear, a gravelly-voiced Native American shaman, came into Paul's body to address my questions. I immediately asked him for information about Sakkara.

Sakkara is a being, like the Earth is a being. It is a different kind of being than you relate to as a personality. It's a matrix, a link to all kinds of sources of energy that are important for each person's awakening. It is a being that nurtures you like the Earth, sun or ocean does. It is a huge being, so huge that if you could see and sense it in its entirety, it might seem overwhelmingly imposing and impersonal.

"Why does Sakkara include geometric symbols and forms?" I asked.

Sakkara is a conscious being that is a spiritual presence much like a Spirit Guide, but it has many forms. As Guides we sometimes come to you in the form of human beings who understand symbols such as words. Words open up consciousness, so it serves our purpose to come in that way. But there is much that needs to be communicated into this world that comes from a plane that is higher than the dimension of mind. From that higher plane, words are no longer the proper symbols to convey understanding and messages.

On this higher level, a crystalline kind of consciousness can be the appropriate construct through which energy, guidance, understanding and healing can be transmitted beyond the level of intellect. This is how Sakkara presents. It makes itself available in forms that people can receive but might or might not recognize. Understand that there are typical ways that Sakkara frequently travels such as pyramids and star tetrahedrons, but it does not like to be limited. It is flexible and able to come in the way that is needed by a given person or a group of people in any moment.

In Sakkara, you are getting outside of pre-existing thinking to find the eternal frequency that is hidden amidst everything. If you link to it long enough emotions surface, the psyche begins to grow and shift, breakthroughs and insights begin to happen and a new paradigm begins to fall into place.

In Sakkara you have an experience, an awakening. Awakening is the purpose of Sakkara. There is nothing esoteric you need to do or be shown, such as some highly secret technique. Nor is there a need to understand very sophisticated theories, even though they can be extremely valuable to your perspective.

Ultimately, there are two important steps in the journey of awakening. The first is to have spiritual experiences that exist outside of your normal frame of reference and that are meaningful. This happens in Sakkara. The second is to make what you realize and grasp applicable to your every day life so that your daily existence changes. You need aspiration, inspiration and action.

When you have a new perception, it is important to speak it so that it does not slip back and vanish into the field of thousands of other thoughts. Often something outside of you causes those hidden realizations to resonate. When consciousness resonates inside of you and causes things outside of you to respond to it, miracles take place. Miracles are simply synchronous events. When you are vibrating at a certain level you cause the atmosphere around you to also resound as well. That's how spiritual power grows.

At this point I interrupted to ask if Sakkara's purpose is the awakening of the planet as a whole as well as individuals. Sun Bear responded:

Yes, that is right. Awakening, or you might call it ascension, is the discovery of what and who you really are. The truth is that each person is a self-contained divine entity that is continually exuding and receiving vibration from the Creator, the Source, the All That Is. When you experience this truth you have awakened to your true or ascendant nature. This pathway is available to all.

The process of awakening and ascension is unique for each entity. It is the experience of one's light being so consistently potent that it works in all situations. One comes to have total faith in the union with God.

You will get to that place many times and you have to keep finding it again and again. That's the work you need to do for ascension. Ascension means that you go into that place in your consciousness that gets answers in accordance with your highest frequencies or upper register: the wise, the kind, the empowering. You access that place so many times that you forget to refer to the other places in consciousness associated with struggle.

When you live in the upper register of your being, whatever you need manifests faster and faster. Ultimately the manifestation becomes instantaneous and miraculous. The moment you think something, the universe immediately brings it to pass. The moment the universe thinks something, you immediately bring it to pass. This can also be called enlightenment.

In the world, many have had to learn boundaries and limitations in order to create safety within which to live because they do not trust. This tendency presupposes that the universe is unsafe. That thought is profoundly strong not only around the Earth but also around many forms of life. To challenge that thought form is to challenge the misbelief that is encoded in many life forms on this planet. It is encoded on the molecular level, in the DNA. The misperception is that life is unsafe and there is a need to be protected. Rather, live life with the absolute certainty that it is safe to be alive in every respect.

Safety comes from merging with infinite boundless form rather than from creating boundaries for protection. This approach to life takes many experiences and revelations to fully comprehend. It also takes being in an experience with oneself and in relationship with others who have glimpsed or are merged in that same totality of safety. Sakkara offers that experience.

When Sun Bear told me that Sakkara was a live being, I realized that it was a conscious matrix of energy, alive with its own consciousness. Understanding this allowed me to relate to Sakkara in a fuller way because I was in an actual relationship with it, as with a lover. I became aware that Sakkara and I worked in concert in what the Guides called the Great Work. Our combined efforts were to help with the shift of the electromagnetic field and the awakening of consciousness occurring on the planet.

After this conversation with Sun Bear, I realized that Sakkara had always been with me. I had never been separate from it. I had simply been working with the diminished version that I could handle at that time. Therefore, the energy that had come through me for my clients and students was, in fact, Sakkara in a stepped down form.

In the beginning there had been only a small flow of its energy available. There had been no identifiable Masters, geometric forms, or intense epiphanies. The verbal messages were not as specific or articulate. As my own consciousness expanded, so did my ability to receive and transmit Sakkara in a more refined, expansive and potent way. My ability to access and transmit the energies of Sakkara went hand in hand with my own awakening.

I had arrived at a watershed moment in my relationship with Sakkara in that I was now more aware of the true nature of the energies I was transmitting for healing and awakening. In response to my awareness, Sakkara was able to present in a fuller form, replete with its exquisite love, power and complexity.

I grew in confidence to invite and transmit Sakkara's energies for groups of people. Previously, I had simply trusted my intuition that something beneficial and transformational was occurring. Now, each time I invoked and transmitted the energies of Sakkara, it revealed more of itself to me.

The more I understood and trusted Sakkara, the more magnetic its attraction became to others. I began to offer Sakkara to larger and larger groups. I found that whether there were twelve or several hundred participants, each person was able to focus on his or her own awakening within the context of the whole gathering while feeling connected to the whole.

Each person's responses to the energies of Sakkara were quite unique. Some would become very still and silent while others would express profound emotions or movement. The common denominator was an expansion in consciousness as each took the next step of his or her own awakening.

Gradually, musicians joined us to play live improvisational music using drums, flute, keyboard, saxophone, kalimba, bells and voice. The music followed the rising and falling tides of Sakkara and added a wonderful element, as did movement. As I continued to offer Sakkara, I noticed that people were experiencing breakthroughs and revelations that previously would have taken weeks, months or even years of one on one work. Thankfully, my new path was unfolding more exquisitely than ever I could have imagined.

CHAPTER 5

MATAARE

Treat the All That Is as your most intimate lover with whom all things are discussed and upon whom you can rely for everything. – Sun Bear

Before receiving Sakkara, I had led energy healing workshops on many topics, including addictions healing. After receiving Sakkara, my desire to offer other workshops vanished. Only Sakkara held my interest. However, there was one addiction healing workshop remaining that was part of a series in Orlando and I decided to honor this commitment, as it would be the last one.

I was packing my suitcase for Orlando when Paul called to tell me that he was in need of a healer. He went on to say that the Guides had suggested that he call me. I was extremely surprised, pleased and more than a little bit nervous about shifting roles. I had come to know the Guides so well through Paul, but I knew nothing about his personal life. Nor did he know anything about mine, because during my readings he was in trance and had no memory of what transpired.

I had come to rely on the Guides through Paul as the main source of my awakening, healing, information and support. What if I couldn't give him what he needed and then he couldn't channel for me anymore? The stakes seemed exceptionally high to risk, but something urged me to say yes. As Paul lived near Orlando, I invited him to my workshop as a guest.

On the morning of the workshop, I met Paul at the front door of the meeting site. While I was delighted to see him, my palms were clammy. I was quite anxious as to whether or not my skills as a healer would meet with his approval.

Since I closely identified Paul with the Guides, I felt I was going to be tested and judged by them as I worked with Paul. If I were judged negatively, I'd lose him and the Guides. Fortunately, I didn't know at the time that Paul was extremely skeptical about healing work, for I would have felt even more pressure to perform.

For the addictions healing workshops, Spirit had given me very specific instructions. First, the participants were asked to picture their addiction. This image brought up a particular kind of energy block in their brains. Then, Spirit would transmit a very specific frequency of light into their heads that would dissolve those blocks. Many people reported immediate relief of their symptoms, claiming that their desire for the substance had disappeared. In many cases, instantly they stopped smoking, drinking coffee, eating sugar or whatever the case might be.

When the workshop was over, Paul reported that during the energy transmission he felt fingers and hands all over his body poking, prodding and rearranging him. I felt relieved that something had occurred for him. This gave me the confidence to audaciously offer him a private healing session right then and there. He very hesitantly agreed.

As we entered Paul's hotel room, I felt even more awkward than I had in the workshop. Paul seemed strangely distant, not too unlike how I had been when I arrived for my first reading with him. He flopped down in a large chair, folded his arms defensively across his chest and peered at me with suspicious skepticism. He told me that he had called me only because the Guides were insistent that he do so, and that while he was open to traditional psychotherapy, he wasn't so sure about this "weird spiritual energy stuff."

I was shocked at his attitude. He was a trance channel, for heaven's sake! Talk about weird spiritual energy stuff! I held my tongue and simply took a deep breath to calm the fears rising within me. I walked over and positioned myself in front of Paul's chair. His extreme skepticism unnerved me, so I closed my eyes for a moment to ask Spirit to help me handle this potentially sticky situation. Instantly, Sakkara's energies came flooding through me in such a torrent that I was almost knocked off my feet. I felt my hands being moved by Spirit and I surrendered into the divine dance. My fear dissipated and I felt the energy transmission penetrating Paul's body. He let out an audible sigh and slumped down in the chair, uncrossing his arms.

I felt the Guides connecting Paul with his true self. They called it a soul healing. Paul and I were simultaneously pulled into the energies by an exquisitely tender yet powerful love. Even though our bodies were not touching, our spirits, our bodies of light were entwined and merged as one. It felt as if we were making love in a way I had never before experienced.

Having previously done many healings, I had certainly experienced stunning energies before. But never had I felt that I was making love to this degree with another being. It seemed that God was directly making love to Paul through me and simultaneously to me through Paul and then us with each other.

When the healing finished I was shaken and embarrassed. I was afraid to tell Paul, a man I barely knew, that I felt as if we had just made love. We had shared an intimate connection that could not be defined in any other way. It was an unconventional twist on the romantic notion of love at first sight.

Many months later, after we had gotten to know each other better personally, Paul and I compared notes. I learned that he had experienced exactly what I had and that it had affected him just as deeply. Paul confided that it was confusing for him as well. He too felt that we had made love and had experienced a romantic intimacy of the most profound kind, much deeper than anything he had known before.

It had been disconcerting for him as well that we didn't know each other. He went on to admit that he had dreamed that a dark haired woman who looked like me would be his true life partner. He wasn't sure, but he thought that perhaps I was that dark haired woman.

Early the next morning after the soul healing, Paul called to say that he had just had an extraordinary experience. While meditating, he clearly heard a voice insistently calling *Mataare! Mataare!* He instinctively knew that this was the voice of God and that he was receiving a divine message. The voice had called the name again and again until Paul realized that Mataare was the true name of his soul.

After this meditation, Paul wrote in his journal, "On September 20, 1992, I experienced a powerful transformative meditation resulting in a major shift in my awareness. The former personality of Paul transcended into my Greater Being, whose name is Mataare. I now experience life as Mataare and no longer feel the same identification with the personality who was Paul. I will now be using Mataare as my name." Without a moment's hesitation, I began to call him Mataare. It rolled off of my tongue naturally, capturing the essence of this soul that I had somehow known for eternity.

When I returned to Boston, I realized that the depth of love I had experienced with Mataare was the same feeling I had experienced with Chief Great White Eagle through Mataare. My mind began to race. The Guides had said that my soul mate would be an aspect of the Chief. Was Mataare in fact my real soul mate?

I was currently in a relationship with a tall dark-haired man named Isaac. I had grown close to him emotionally, but he did not touch my heart and soul the way Mataare did and I craved that kind of depth. I wanted to be touched so deeply that doubt and uncertainty would disappear as I was transported into divine love. I wanted a man with Chief Great White Eagle's calm, powerful, and confident masculinity.

Despite Mataare's dream about the dark haired woman, it didn't seem to me that Mataare was my true partner. He didn't match the image I had dreamed. Physically, we didn't fit well together and our personalities were so extremely opposite that I didn't see how we could possibly get along. I imagined that we would constantly be on each other's nerves because of the differences in our preferences and approaches to life.

Despite these radical differences, there was something between us so compellingly electric, attractive and magnetic that we were drawn together. I thought about Mataare incessantly. When we spoke on the phone, I felt an explosion of consuming flames throughout my body. It was as if he were able to ignite my whole being into an enhanced reality. We were one organism, united in an eternal dance of passionate, expansive, timeless communion. Yet it seemed odd to have this intimate connection without the usual ingredients present.

Desperate for clarity about our relationship, I decided to ask the Guides for insight. It seemed strange to ask the Guides through Mataare about Mataare, because the subject was the medium. However, since he would not personally be there anyway once the Guides arrived, I reasoned, there was no need for concern.

We have stuck a Mataare in your life and an Anamika in his life to create an environment where love can grow. The growth of your spirits takes place powerfully in each other's presence. Yet, you must deeply appreciate what is now and let go of what is not now. That is a lesson that you need to learn to remember.

I wasn't happy with their enigmatic answer. It left me hanging and uncertain. I hated it when the Guides didn't really answer my question in a concrete way but just gave me the spiritual lesson. It brought out a frustrated impetuous child in me who wanted her need met *now*. I wanted them to tell me definitively whether or not Mataare was my true partner, even though I didn't think he was. I felt a deep eternal bond between our souls, even though our personal journey in this life had just begun. I was very confused, because unlike his dark haired dream lover, my dream lover did not resemble Mataare at all. Mine always appeared as a tall, blue-eyed man.

You are involved in an experience where you are coming closer to your soul mate. You are getting more understanding about it but you are not yet at the point where it happens. There is nothing wrong. You need to accept that this is where you are now. You are being shown something very beautiful and important about how to be, rather than how to accomplish. This lesson is something you have had to teach yourself because your family and culture didn't teach it to you. You were taught that if you accomplish and achieve, you could get some reward.

The energy you are looking for from a relationship is actually within you. Sometimes you have felt that energy in the presence of a person like Mataare, so you have thought that the energy must be related to the person. Instead, what happens is that you open up to a part of yourself in the presence of that person. You have to be living in that presence with many people before it can happen with THE person. What I am talking about is being in a successful relationship with the universe and with yourself so that you are most often in ecstasy with your life. Finding that state of being within yourself is what mastery is all about.

Relieved to have received a more direct and satisfying answer, I was still hungry to know more about my soul mate. I persisted, "This morning as I was walking through a field with Shamuki, I felt a beam pierce my heart. It seemed to come from a person whom I have not yet met.

I stopped abruptly and saw a well-shaped pair of male hands reach to me through the ethers. The hands were not quite physically there, but were almost palpable. I reached to take his hands. As I did, I felt his spirit body merge with my physical body as if we began to make love. It was as strong and real as if he were there physically. This was a very beautiful experience."

It has already happened in another dimension and it will occur in the physical as well. You need to understand that soul mate is not a single physical being but a kind of spirit being who is always alerting you to the presence and to his arrival.

The person you will choose who is right for you can only come when you are more in your soul's purpose. In the meantime, enjoy who is near you now. It is very simple to allow this greater level of expansion to come. It is as simple as allowing your devotion toward God and toward the universe to rise up within you. Treat the All That Is as your most intimate lover with whom all things are discussed and upon whom you can rely for everything. If this dimension of self is opened so that your higher self is received as a lover, then you shall find a growing peace. Then, all that is meant to come to you can come.

Enjoying 'now' brings contentment to the child part of you, which needs to know that that which she desires is important and accessible. As you develop, this inner child will shift from being the child to being a co-creator in existence.

The Guides' presence lifted me out of my relentlessly questioning mind and put me into the embrace of the great love once again. I let go and opened my body to feel their words:

You are developing a romance with the Divine, which is more splendid than any other. Becoming a lover of the Supreme depends on your willingness to love. This is the stage you are currently in, embracing your power and greatness through humility, which is gratitude. You are aligned with the highest source of power in existence. True power as you know, exists in its highest form as love or light. There is no other power in truth but that which is love and light.

Enjoy devotion, longing, and fullness, for you will see that these only build intimacy between you and the Divine. When you look into the mirror you will see the face of the Beloved in you. You will see how your sincere heart calls to the Spirit of the Divine and embraces it. You will see how loved you are, how the Divine lives in you and holds you as a precious jewel, the jewel that you truly are.

I basked in the warmth of the comforting energy of the Guides. I could for the moment let go of my need to know who my soul mate was. I understood that the most important thing to me right now was truly my own journey of awakening. For the moment, I could let everything else just be.

I also knew something else: Mataare was on this journey too and whatever unfolded from here on, we were in it together.

CHAPTER 6

The God Ring

There is a passion flame, a fire, a burning so strong that all you wish to do is to love, to offer thanks and to commune with it in a divine and sacred intertwining. – Yeshua

I began to hear stories about various Avatars such as Sai Baba, Ammachi, and Mother Meera. People were flocking to see them, recommending that I go too. Friends filled me with stories and books about their lives. Hearing their names again and again seemed to be a message that I needed to go see them. With each passing day it became more difficult to ignore the call.

Sai Baba began showing up in dreams and visions. I would feel an exchange of energy with him as he called me to come to him. I wanted to heed this call, but was too sick to make the long journey to India. I did mange to see Ammachi. Her compassion was beautiful as she hugged and blessed person after person. Then, I went to Germany to see Mother Meera. She sat on her throne in silence. One by one people would sit at her feet for a few moments to receive her energy which was pure, clean and transformative.

I left each one with the same unusual urgency of wanting to know these Avatars on a human level, because as people they seemed so remote. I could feel the beauty of their transmission, but I could detect little of who they were as real people and nothing of their personal lives. Did they have lovers? Did they live alone? Did they sleep or meditate much? What did they eat? Did they take nutritional supplements? Did they have aches, pains and illness? Did they feel happy when they were not working? Did they feel lonely or empty? What did they yearn for if anything? I had all of these questions and more.

I couldn't reconcile the fact that I had an extraordinary gift of energy transmission too, but I was a regular person. I had the mistaken notion that an Avatar is beyond human and cannot live fully engaged in the world. It appeared to me that they had in effect traded their worldly sensibilities for spiritual ones. It also seemed to me that this trade-off was mandatory, because I erroneously believed that to become more spiritual one must become less human.

I had so many mistaken notions about what it meant to be spiritual or enlightened or an Avatar. My images were of people who were perfect, mysterious, and not dealing with the daily challenges I encountered. It seemed that to be successful spiritually it would be necessary to abstract my essence from the day-to-day life that had always defined and vitalized me while I committed to a higher ideal so that the cost on a personal level would be total and absolute. I feared that to awaken spiritually I would have to become more perfect and less myself. Possessing a personality and enjoying life on Earth seemed a detriment to spiritual ascendancy.

Needless to say, if all this were true, then I was quite spiritually deficient. I delighted far too much in the human experience from all of my friends, Shamuki, Isaac to music and on and on. In addition, I seemed to have so much personal baggage to clean up.

These experiences with the Avatars also left me confused because their way of working with transmission was so similar to Sakkara. If I could invoke Sakkara, I reasoned, did that mean I was just like them? To me it didn't seem I was anything like these ones who seemed the epitome of spiritual existence. Compared to them I felt like a gypsy, like Carmen working in a cigarette factory. I was quite perplexed by the seeming contradiction of a transmission of love as potent as Sakkara coming through me and yet I didn't fit any spiritual mold. How could such a profoundly awakening energy that changed everything in its path come through someone who wasn't a spiritual leader and wasn't removed from worldly affairs?

Needless to say, I was very confused about what spirituality really was, and I was riddled with images of a false nature. When I returned home from each visit to the Avatars, I felt like a failure since everyone knew they had extraordinary healing powers, yet I couldn't surrender to follow them as so many others did. This must be some deficiency on my part, I concluded.

I did much soul searching until I finally came to realize that I had to be true to my own imperatives and they were not calling me to be a disciple of any teacher in particular or to be a guru myself. When I reviewed my experiences of seeing many of them in action, I noticed that they were comfortable with and trusting of their energy transmissions. This gave me added courage to trust the transmissions of Sakkara even more. Instinctively, I knew that Sakkara was a force of profound good, but every time I offered its energy, I was plagued with profound doubts. Will the energy come through me this time? Will people benefit from the experience? Will the energies be strong enough, good enough, wise enough, loving enough?

Seeking clarity, I called Mataare to arrange a session with the Guides in hopes that they could explain to me who I was and how to be both spiritual and human. This time, the voice that came to address me was Miriam, the mother of Yeshua, known to the world as Mary. She epitomized gentle compassion.

"What is an Avatar?" I asked her.

An Avatar is one who is absolutely committed to and has merged in their truth.

I asked, "Is it possible to become an Avatar or do you have to be born that way?" I was certain that I wasn't one if I had to be born that way. Yet, I felt such a powerful soul resonance with the work of the Avatars despite what I perceived to be my spiritual deficiencies. It was as if we were here to do the same thing, just in a different way.

Avatars are born with the consciousness they are here to transmit. However, Avatars are not always born in their mastery. Mastery often needs to be developed. Avatars eventually awaken to Truth even when not knowing the way. They still go through their lessons and many may be completely baffled by the world into which they are born. Nevertheless, they do not accept any of the teachings of the world over the teachings they know inside.

"It seems that during this period of the earth's history that there is more support for awakening than ever before."

In the last 50-100 years there has been tremendous breakthrough in this world, greater than in any other time in the history of human development. Collectively, the advances made in the last fifty years alone are more than in all of the last one million years. So quick is the rate of development of mind and intellect inspired from the spiritual dimensions, that they require a spiritual awakening to happen.

There are two guiding intelligences: that of the mind and that of the heart or spirit. It must be the spirit which guides the intellect or it shall lead to the unraveling of all civilization here on Earth. To guide this development, Spirit has drawn very near to this plane so that those who wish to may more easily access their spiritual nature. Our true purpose is to link all those who wish to the same Source with which we are linked. We remove ourselves at that juncture.

"Yes, I've noticed that more and more people are interested in spiritual matters as well and are growing rapidly. But some also seem to fall by the wayside."

There shall be many in this world who do not utilize the energies to which they have awakened. Many shall abuse the gift that has awakened within them. It is their privilege to use the gift in any way they choose. Even if it is misused, it is their gift.

"What about my quandary regarding being spiritual and human?"

One must be able to maintain one's own unique identity as well as one's merged identity. People who are a vehicle of the light in this world must be prepared to be absolutely extraordinary and unlimited and also to be absolutely ordinary and small. This paradox exists. One who walks the realms between worlds, as you do, needs to learn to be at peace with this dichotomy. We are glad for the awakening that unfolds in you and we are proud of how you use your gifts. We are glad you offer them so freely with so much openness and love.

I edged closer to one of my currently consuming questions. "I have so many fears and so much self-doubt that I'm afraid that the gift of Sakkara might leave me and that I will never fulfill my destiny. How could I possibly be a spiritual person with all of this fear?"

You were born with the consciousness that you are here to transmit. You will develop your fully awakened nature; it is your path. To accomplish this you were given a very powerful gift, Sakkara. It is a gift given to you by the Divine, and you have given it to others selflessly. It is not because you are entirely free of fear-based needs or motivations. Rather, even though you have only some comprehension of the gift, you have nonetheless trusted that your gift is good. You have shown a willingness to give of it to others even before totally understanding it. You have fully accepted that you wish to give of this since you have understood it to somehow be part of a divine plan for you.

Her response elated me and I thought about what that really meant for my life. I realized that it did not mean becoming a guru or having thousands of people sit at my feet the way others did it. It meant claiming the most real part of me. It meant learning to walk my highest path in each moment. It meant growing ever more compassionate and full of love. It meant accepting my humanity commingled with my divinity, holding the awareness that one did not contradict the other. It meant awakening to what everyone is inherently, a unique aspect of divine love and letting that light shine in the world.

After the conversation with Miriam I began to see visions of gold – everywhere, gold. When I meditated I would see a soft white gold light. When I was working with individuals, I would feel gold surrounding us. During Sakkara, a golden mist showered the room. When I looked at Shamuki, whose fur was golden, he would be bathed in golden light. When I closed my eyes to sleep, a golden wave ushered in my dreams. I began to think that I was seeing visions of my true home. Perhaps I had come from a gold planet. When I asked the Guides about it they laughingly informed me that I was not from a golden planet, but from the golden ray.

Intrigued but ignorant, I asked for an explanation about what they meant by the golden ray. They explained that the golden ray is the ninth ray, a very high frequency. They said that a high frequency ray was not better than rays of other colors. View the rays, they instructed, as notes on a scale, high or low in frequency. I wanted to know what color the God ray would be. I was told that it was comprised of all the colors and was therefore colorless. Wondering how I could reach the God ray, I was told that if I embraced all of the rays fully they would explode into the colorless or God ray.

I fervently wanted to achieve this, but wasn't sure exactly how. The Guides explained that there was nothing I needed to do to get there. They went on to say that in our natural state, we are all in the God ray. It is only our perception that we are not there. A revelation started taking shape for me – all souls are in the God ray, yet we have sent pieces of our consciousness into different densities to learn certain things. Thus, all we need to do is let go of the struggle and suffering and wake up to the truth that we are already there!

Prior to this revelation I had been living as if there was some hierarchy or stages I had to work through like climbing the corporate ladder to find my God self. With this new awareness, it felt like a shell was cracked, as if a veil of blindness slipped off and I began to merge even more with my true self. Total bliss does not even begin to describe the sensation. I wish I could say that this awareness stayed with me, but at the time, I slipped in and out of it.

I began to have more and more visions of white gold and was feeling an impulse to perform some sort of ceremony to solidify my feeling of oneness. In one of these visions I saw a white gold ring with seven diamonds. I approached a jeweler to have the ring made, insisting that it be ready by October 13th, my fortieth birthday.

The ceremony to unite myself with God began to take shape in my mind. My intention was to increase my trust and commitment, as if I were marrying God. My connection with what felt like God had increased to the extent that now I was eager to pledge myself in union to this Source of existence. Yet, God was still not personal for me. That was to come later.

Mataare called unexpectedly on October 12th, his voice full of mystery. He announced that he would be flying up the next day for my birthday. "Exciting things are afoot," he said without explaining further what he meant. I was thrilled he was coming and I had to agree that something unusual was up.

On the day of my birthday, I awoke with a feeling of great anticipation. My first priority was to rush to the jewelers. I waited expectantly as he brought out the box containing the ring. My design turned out beautifully: three white gold rings nestled together perfectly to comprise one large ring. There were seven little diamonds asymmetrically placed around one large mine-cut diamond in the middle, symbolizing the One. It shone magically in the light. With a high heart, I snapped the box shut, not to be reopened again until later that night in the union ceremony. On the way home, I impulsively bought six white roses for the occasion.

As the evening neared, Mataare arrived. When I opened the door, he was standing there with six white roses in one hand and a ring box in the other. My mouth dropped open as I virtually yanked him into the house, insisting that he open his ring box. There, nestled in the blue velvet was a white gold ring with many diamonds. He told me that he had been impelled to buy this ring for himself for some kind of ceremony to symbolize his union with God. A comparison of the numerous visions we had received leading up to this synchronous event clued us in that the Guides were definitely up to something. We surmised that they were inspiring us to do this ceremony for some reason. Although neither of us had the slightest idea what would come of it, we were both committed.

As the time for the ceremony drew near, a few special friends arrived to bear witness. Each was given a white rose. Mataare and I both affirmed that our ceremony was a symbolic union with God. We affirmed our intention to know the Source ever more intimately. Sensing that the Guides wished to add to the ceremony, Mataare slipped effortlessly into trance. This time, no ohms were required.

It was Miriam who spoke. *It is time for human beings to discover their own inherent divinity and allow that to come to the fore. There are many that call upon the Creator, if they believe in one, and beg for intervention. There are some that would pray for the end to come and for all evils to be smitten. Such things show disturbing misunderstanding of the nature of truth and God.*

The name of God is "God." The name is not a title. The name of God is a vibration, it is a living force that inspires one to remember and surrender. This name of God will grow in you more and more and become alive in you. You become one with the name and the name becomes one with you. It is a sacred and ineffable name that is a living presence that is remembrance.

God does not wish you to believe in God, but rather to know God. Beliefs stand in the way of the knowledge of God, the Source, by direct experience. There are some that put off such knowledge and experience for life after life. There are others who would even say that God can never be known. The source of true suffering is the belief that God is far away, apart, unknowable and unreachable. This causes a sense of great dissociation from all that matters and leads to the supreme pain and hurt that people fear about existing.

Beliefs in God can sometimes be helpful, but God does not seek your belief. We, as agents of God, do not seek your belief in us either. Rather, we urge your direct experience of that which is the Source, for that is available to you. How does one know this Source? You must first be interested in it. Knowledge of self also leads to the heart of God, for each soul is an aspect of the Creator. He or she that learns their true self shall also come to know the Creator.

Merely by having the intent to contact the Source of All, there shall come a guidance that draws near to you. If you would search to know God first, then all other matters in your life shall begin to unfold with more and more grace. There may need to be a great deal that must first be unraveled. As you get closer to the Source, there may be many elements in your life which have been born of feeling separated from the Source. There may be many involvements, which you may be holding onto desperately as if they are the source of your survival, when they just might be the source of your pain.

When you welcome the Source into your life, change begins. Some things fall apart. Know that something else is being restructured so that your life may be based upon that which truly nurtures and prospers you. All that you may have clung to out of limited beliefs shall then dissipate. You shall be given that which is beyond your own ability to create, even though you shall participate with its very creation.

There was a long pause and the energy shifted ever so slightly. Mataare's voice, which had sounded like a woman filled with divine love, transformed to a man's voice with a strong resemblance to Miriam. My heart swelled with love as I recognized her son, Yeshua.

The greater light does not unfold because of aspiration, but rather because of devotion. There is a passion flame, a fire, a burning so strong, that all you wish to do is to love, to offer thanks and to commune with it in a divine and sacred intertwining.

The devotion, you see, is a gift. It is given in a simple way with a prayer. This prayer is offered because there are times when your being feels as though it forgets or pulls away from the truth of its light. This separation becomes so painful that one begins to pray to always be in the remembrance of love. This is where the devotion begins. Yours has already begun and to many others this may seem like obsession. But to the one amidst the experience, it is joy. It is the light itself.

This devotion and single-mindedness bring the whole body into the light. They are born of prayer or dialogue with the heavens. It is that which puts you on track. It is the dialogue inwardly between you and the Infinite which says, "Infinite One, join me with you, my heart aches at the separation and dance in joy at the union."

62-Into the Heart of the Beloved

These prayers come from deep in your being and in your soul. They are offered up because there is nothing else which feels as important. They remove the need for disciplines in practice because they create a passion for the path. Then one need not have the rigor of discipline in order to stay on the path. All you need is to let the love and devotion grow on their own.

There is a journey that all souls make. The journey is from not even knowing you exist to total consciousness that you exist. In that place you are in an interplay and interaction with all of the higher forces. In order for you to join those forces which know themselves as eternal, you must also embrace the truth that you are eternal.

Life is about both becoming the master of your existence and being one who is also surrendered to a higher power. All of this is extremely easy and totally effortless. When you are in that place of entwining with the Cosmic Will, your will and Cosmic Will are one. Cosmic intention becomes your intention. If you need our help, invite us, but do not conjure. Begging and pleading are not necessary, just devotion. The Supreme, like us, responds to devotion more than anything else.

I let myself melt into the consummate love I always felt in the presence of the Guides. I dissolved into the fullness of my heart and sensed God entering. Mataare gently came out of trance. While not remembering the exact words, he too felt the presence of God in his heart. We were held in the sacredness of the moment as we sat in silence looking at each other. We had both taken vows of union with our own inner Divine Source. We had shared something beautiful and sacred.

Without speaking a word, we both reached for the boxes that held our rings. Mataare ceremoniously placed my ring on the ring finger of my left hand. I did the same for him. In so doing, we were not only symbolically wed to the Divine, but were pledged to each other as soul mates for eternity, companions in our journey of the One.

CHAPTER 7

THE DOORWAY

To receive your soul mate you must make an intimate lover of the universe. True peace comes from the acceptance and total appreciation of everything that you are and of everything that is around you right now. – Philos

The idea of a more personal and intimate relationship with God was thrilling and I was eager for it to happen. In this process the Guides had much to teach me. I kept their words in focus as if I were an athlete training for my first marathon and they were my coaches.

Greetings to you, my friend, it is Philos. I am the Keeper of the Akashic Records. Akasha is a record of all that ever was and shall be in this universe: all that is now, all that exists now as potential, all which may have been, all which might be, as well as all parallel existences to this one.

Our communions are to help you shift into your expanded self, so that you may know the truth of why you exist and live in fulfillment. You are here to experience love and a divine expression of life so beautiful it is impossible to describe. You are here to live in dimensions of beauty and light so numerous that living in the human body is but one tiny part of that entire realm of experience. Your natural state, dear Anamika, is a state of love. The time comes when all feelings and emotions come within this context so securely and safely that you rest permanently in love. This is the doorway that has arrived so that you may enter it.

Philos was speaking to the part of me that knew that awakening was the only real path for me. By the same token, I didn't feel the way I thought I should. I wasn't sure what an awakened state felt like, but I knew it wasn't how I felt at that time.

I had been consciously working on myself since I was a small child. At nineteen I became involved in a peer counseling movement in which we learned both counseling and clienting skills. The recommendation was that each person give and receive one session per week. I would regularly give and receive six. That's how fervent, eager, devoted and passionate I was about my awakening. I had kept up that pace for fifteen years and as such had been able to clear out quite a bit of internal baggage.

After all of this, I was perplexed and infuriated that I had still not arrived. I was still unable to consistently access the great love I craved. I still had not been able to fulfill my dreams of life partnership and a powerful unfolding of life purpose the way I imagined it to be.

I know now that I had no conception of the amount of work I had yet to face. It was fortunate that I didn't know the extent of it because the task would have been daunting.

There is a thief that can rob you while you are in your natural state of beauty and light. The thief is an old self-created pattern, thought, belief system or energy form that leaves you feeling that something is wrong. Prior to its arrival you were in perfection. Recognize that any perception of harm that leaves you feeling disempowered is not reality but illusion. There is one and only one focus that can bring the sense of rightness; that is again and again returning to the point of love. It is an empowered and beautiful state.

Your spirit is seeking freedom of the ultimate kind and is challenged by fears. Your fear is ultimately a fear of your inability to survive. It is a fear of death, of the end. What will actually end is one and only one thing, a perception called ego or identity. You are not doing this life for reputation, for your ego, or because you need to feel important. You are living here, doing all that you are doing for love's sake. In those moments that you are giving and experiencing love, you will be perfect and healed. You will be in your reason for existence and in joy. Then you will find that the outer world simply doesn't matter as much to you any more. It cannot hurt you and you will not fear it.

This takes one simple thing, remembering to see through fear to the truth. This doorway that I speak of is the very doorway about which you have asked us. You have been knocking on it for a long time. More and more of these doorways will be visible to you and your veils will be lifted until all you see is what is real.

"That is easier said than done," I thought. Somehow it seemed that I had spent more time with the thief than in the beauty. As Philos was presenting this doorway to me I became aware of the depth of terror that still resided in me. I didn't know what it was about, but I knew that there was some deep darkness lurking in crevices into which I could fall if I wasn't careful. I feared this horrifying abyss for I felt that it could destroy me.

Simultaneously, I began to sense the possibility of opening into other dimensions, dimensions that were very light and beautiful. I sensed that I was way up on the mountain and if I could get through the doorway all would be beautiful. However, if I didn't, it was a long way down. In an instant I could be in heaven or in hell.

This terror that I felt seemed both personal and collective. I couldn't separate them. Some of it felt like a universal void, nothingness while some of it was a personal hell, fueled by my fear that there really is no love, only loss.

Your might and power come from seeing where you can let go and choosing to do so. Then, nothing has power over you anymore. Each time you let go you are releasing a part of your former identity. That can be a little frightening because you are letting go of something that took a long time to construct.

Your gift is not merely allowing Spirit to come through you, but rather your attunement to Spirit. You vibrate at the same frequency as Spirit, which lets us flow through you. You are not an empty vessel and Spirit the juice.

With this simple statement, I understood that the healing work with which I was engaged was indeed raising my vibration. I was resonating with higher and higher frequencies, gaining greater and greater access to a multidimensional reality. The more I acknowledged and accepted my fears, the more my awareness of love grew. These fears were keys to the doorway of love.

Even though Philos said that I wasn't just some empty receptacle for Spirit to fill and that I was, in fact, vibrating there, I still felt a long way from the deep peace, love and acceptance I imagined possible. Despite the Guides' continual reassurance, I still did not have my soul mate or the fullness of my mission. No matter how hard I tried, no matter how many lessons I learned, my two primary dreams remained unmet. I couldn't cope with this. Patiently, the Guides kept trying to enlighten me:

To receive your soul mate you must make an intimate lover of the universe. True peace comes from the acceptance and total appreciation of everything that you are and of everything that is around you right now. This includes the gamut of emotions, feelings and inspirations. When one has this level of peace there is a faith, a trust, an inherent safety and a joy at being in this moment. This is a state of no judgment. It is simply a state of experience. Complete and total acceptance allows any entity to go onward into the next dimension.

True growth takes place in the passion, feeling, presence, and prescience of the moment. In this state of being, all of one's needs are met. As soon as there is an urge, there is an opportunity to fulfill the urge so that no lingering need remains. This only exists when a being has found unconditional and unlimited acceptance, or love.

Recently, you have moved into a level where you are in preparation for that God union you desire. This is the state of being of soul mate. This is a state of being where one is in an intercourse with the universal force of fulfillment. That force has a way of causing the world to look fulfilling in every respect. It draws you into partnership. You must learn how to consistently embrace this magnificent union as a part of the pattern of your being. This is a training for life, and life is a training to enter that most sacred embrace.

There are two aspects to the Supreme Divinity: darkness and light. Without the void there would be no place for the light to appear. Without the light, there would be nothing in the darkness. You must embrace the light as well as the void or blackness. That's what all of this healing work is about, not fearing the negative emotions and also embracing the dark. In the void is also expansion. Avoid the void and you avoid expansion. When you see the void, you have a journey to make.

If you wish the embrace of the Source then love and devotion are needed. You must let the part of your being which cannot bear another moment of separation come forward. This must be directed towards the invisible but very present force of God, which is love. This longing is not to be pushed away but felt, for from it comes prayer, from prayer comes devotion and from devotion comes union.

The heart cannot bear the pain of separation and yearns to dwell in the place beyond all imagining. There have been years of challenge, struggle, suffering, pain, effort and surviving. Now it is time to rest, to rest in divine love, in the nurture of the One, the Supreme, the beloved devotion flame.

Every feeling, emotion and thought is important. This is how you make a lover of the universe. You must talk with the universe as though it were your lover. Speak from a place of love deep inside you, rather than a place of being squeezed into doing it. To be a lover you need dialogue or conscious prayer. The intimacy therein developed brings a greater level of ease into the spirit and into life. Ease brings in greater levels of resources and causes you to be an even better catalyst for the people around you. The focus for you now simply needs to be, "I am ready to have a life of ease."

"Oh, I just want it now," I sighed in exasperation. "This waiting and waiting is so painful. Can't you speed things up for me?"

Pain comes from the perception that what you want is missing from your life right now. That is a negative judgment that is robbing you of the pleasure of now. Our intention is to help you be in ecstasy. Ecstasy draws in many things including a soul mate. A part of ecstasy is even finding the richness of negative emotions. You must remember that it really isn't a soul mate that can fill that place. It is love itself, not a person. If you were in the right inner place, love would be forthcoming from anyone because you have found the place that draws what you need from life. The shift is one that is inside of you. You are trying to embrace such great levels of light that you are able to easily connect with whatever you must learn or seek out. You see how you are allowing your fears to surface as we speak?

Philos was right. I could indeed feel great fears rising up in my being.

Whatever you no longer have need for, let it go into the light and ask that it be taken. The Archangel Mikael will be present with you and will cut the ties with those fears with his blue sword. Allow Mikael to take his sword and cut the tie between you and your fear. Put your hand on the sword as he cuts it. Mikael now carries away that energy form which you no longer need into the light.

As Philos was speaking, I saw a bright blue sword that I subsequently learned is the signature of Archangel Mikael. I instantly felt much lighter. "Yes, the fear is lifting. But, Philos, I still feel empty. I wish something could infuse me and fill the emptiness which has replaced the fear."

Let Mikael embrace you, all of you, Anamika. Let Mikael completely merge with you.

It was easy to do what he instructed. I relaxed my body and allowed Mikael's exquisite energy to fill me more deeply.

Yes, now you are receiving Mikael. Choose to give yourself freely. It is likely that he shall bring you an embrace of total intimacy, including your sexual nature. For in that way you will be in union with his force and he with yours.

As Philos was speaking, I suddenly felt Mikael making love to me. He filled me with his tender yet potent essence. His maleness far surpassed anything I had ever before experienced. Suddenly remembering that Philos was present, I flushed in embarrassment. As foolish as it was to wish there was really was something called privacy, I had to ignore Philos to turn back to Mikael.

Lost in Mikael's embrace, I marveled at the miraculous nature of this universe. For years I had been focusing on a man as a soul mate because I had known nothing else. Here I was experiencing an intimate connection and union in a way I never could have imagined. The Guides had orchestrated a love experience that taught me that reality certainly encompassed more wonderful and extraordinary possibilities than I had known.

The angels always seek to blend with all aspects of your being and share their great gift of power and light. Take Mikael's energy in the place of the fear you released which used to occupy your heart. He seeks to give you part of himself to keep there instead. He shall be with you when you need, integrated and part of your being.

I closed my eyes and took a deep breath, allowing myself to be filled with the love I felt from Philos, from Mikael, and from all the Guides. Gentle peace descended upon me and the pain was lifted.

68-Into the Heart of the Beloved

"The burden has lifted and I feel at peace and in love. How can I hold this, Philos?" I queried anxiously.

You have seen it, you have focused on it and you are in the process of becoming more in attunement with it. Don't worry about tomorrow, just hold it now.

CHAPTER 8

BUDDHA'S ALLERGY

There is no point to existence save love.
All other powers are there but
at best are grains without love.
Love is the power that nurtures
and gives meaning to every dimension. – Philos

I became even more obsessed with enlightenment and could do nothing but meditate for four, five and six hours at a time. Previously, I had never engaged in any formal meditation for even five minutes. Now, I found myself sitting for hours on end, driven by a fierce determination to obtain enlightenment as if it were a goal that could be achieved once and for all.

Previously, the only time I sat still was with my clients, engaged in a sort of meditation in which I held a single-pointed focus for eight to twelve hours a day, allowing Spirit to move through me. Sitting now had a different quality. I felt pulled within, with so many sensations rushing through my body, I was compelled to be with this process to the exclusion of other activities. Drawn by the light that guided me, I plunged deeper and deeper into the darkness.

Rushes of energy consumed me, coursing through my body like torrential rivers and I cried from the beauty and the fear of the unknown. I felt grabbed, as if strong hands held me in an invisible vice and I couldn't move. Sometimes those hands would rock me back and forth as if I were being pushed and pulled. I had no control over my movements and would often end up flat on the floor as if I were being forced to surrender to a power far greater than myself.

I had yearned for this power to consume me and draw me into its embrace. It conveyed such a sure strength that I felt safe to let go in ecstatic abandon. As I surrendered, this powerful force tenderly but insistently penetrated to my very core. I felt touched to the depth of my being. Whatever this was knew everything about me and held no judgment. I could have no secrets or anything to withhold. This was the unconditional love I had yearned for my whole life and I wanted nothing more than to totally surrender into its cradling and penetrating arms.

Was this enlightenment? I didn't know. Whatever it was, I was in heaven, and I was hell-bent on getting more. So I persisted. Yet, as these energies continued day after day, hour after hour, I began to feel irritable and tense. The intensity kept building, but with no release and I desperately sought relief. I was going wild, about to scream or jump out of my skin if something didn't break through. At my wit's end, I called the Guides.

Greeting to you friend, it is Philos.

"Oh, Philos, things are moving so quickly. I thank you for your assistance with that, but I request even further acceleration so I can get this over with."

What results are you looking for? He spoke calmly, which infuriated and inflamed me even further.

"Total enlightenment immediately. I am about to jump out of my skin! Since our last session I've experienced profound meditations and a lot more love. My frustration is that I feel I am not too far from some sort of realization but there is something I can't quite move through yet. What do I need to do to pierce through into complete enlightenment?"

It would be simpler for me to understand what you are asking if you would describe for me what you are calling enlightenment.

"A state of total God realization, a state of complete union with the Divine, a state of... whatever it is that enlightened beings have."

That is very honest of you. Whatever it is, you want it.

"Yes! But I don't know how to describe it since I haven't been there. I only have pieces."

I wonder what it is that you are thinking that they have.

"To be living in a state of profound union and unconditional love all the time. Isn't that what enlightenment is?"

What you describe cannot be attained through increased desire and aspiration. Yet you must have the aspiration in order to attain it. There is a paradox here. When you are merged with All That Is, there is a great power that flows through you, but you don't direct it and it doesn't direct you. It comes from a total appreciation of the moment. Through this appreciation, you could live and express in very ordinary ways while at other times the extraordinary manifests itself within and even around you.

This is not a function of time or speeding up. It is a function of how present you allow yourself to be. Presence comes from a total acceptance of what is now and not looking for anything else. It is a kind of paradox where all that you must do is accept.

You are conscious to some extent of the power that flows through you as it moves to create healings. I assume that when you say enlightenment you are speaking of an increased ability to raise the level of energy to your satisfaction as needed. I do not call that enlightenment. That is a yogic skill.

Enlightenment is total appreciation, without struggle, of what is going on in your existence right now. It's the acceptance of wherever you are, while you are also becoming what you are becoming. It is having a sense of peace about now and about the process of life.

"Then I'm really talking about more total acceptance and peace. Is what I'm searching for ascendancy and not enlightenment?"

I would describe ascendancy as the result of living an enlightened life as an enlightened being. From being at peace with right now and being at peace about growing into what you are becoming, you ascend. The speeding up and slowing down of time are both perceptions outside of ascendant awareness.

If I can help you experience what your ascendancy really means, I would say you embrace infinity and surrender all perceptions of time. When you are in this infinite place it is so different than the perceptions of those in your world. When you live in that infinite place, your world is literally different from others. Those who step into your world enter into a miraculous existence. It is an experience of love that is so intense that it is chosen over and over again. Ascendancy comes by welcoming the challenges and then being prepared to enthusiastically take them on knowing that they are your opportunity to let go of the stresses, to experience the love that is life and that is who you are.

I understand your desire to do this quickly because you are experiencing the rough edges of the ungracious way that you are embracing your light. Realize that what you are looking for is not out of your reach, but already here with you now. If anything at all is slowing you down, if we must choose this terminology, it is the perception that somehow you are outside of it now. The illusions you must break down at all costs are that you are outside of your ascendancy or need other than what is happening right now.

The restlessness and the feeling of jumping out of your skin you have expressed are entirely typical. You reflect much of the allergy that the Buddha did just before he reached his enlightenment. The Buddha was in great pain from exactly the thing that causes you pain. He was endlessly working on himself. He went from Master to Master perfecting different techniques of self-realization and do you know something? He didn't feel any better. But all of the other Master's disciples who watched how perfectly he practiced these techniques became very impressed with him and would ask him what was special about him. He would call them fools. 'Don't you see none of this works? I practiced all of these techniques and still I am miserable.'

He was so distressed, disappointed and hateful towards the Creator for torturing him with no peace even though he did all the things that these Masters would say. He finally decided he was going to die, merge into the light and in essence have a talk with God about His system. Ironically, by that time he had come to believe that it was wrong to kill anything, including himself, so he had a dilemma. He decided that he was simply not going to take any food and water and would just meditate until death. But by that time he had become such a yogi with his practices that he wouldn't die when he meditated. Now he was in an extraordinary dilemma.

To try and solve it he meditated and meditated and would not move. And do you know something? He attained enlightenment. For him, the great realization was that his problem was guilt. He thought that he was being made to suffer because something was incredibly wrong with him, so he strove for perfection.

When he meditated, he found his beauty. That beauty made him realize: 'I was mistaken. I'm not horrible, I'm beautiful. I understand now, I understand! I don't have to do anything, I'm beautiful as I am!' He conceded this so deeply down in his heart that he achieved what had been alluding him.

After his realization, the Buddha went to find all of those monks who had wanted to follow him before who he had shunned and from whom he had turned away. They said, 'Well, maybe you're beautiful, you've always been special. But tell us, what did you really do Bodhisattva?'

He could not get them to believe that they didn't have to do anything. He figured, "Maybe if I get them to do what I did they'll have the same revelation I had." So he essentially tortured them with disciplines. Some of them did realize it but they could not achieve any of the disciplines. When they achieved some he would give them more and make them harder until eventually they would give up and surrender. That was his way of teaching.

The pain that is occurring in you is the pain of purging yourself rather than accepting yourself. This is what we speak of when we say a psychic change is needed. You must have that change which comes from seeking spiritual experience and carrying the message. During this process you are transformed by the Creator, not by your desire to perfect yourself. But, by seeking that, gifts are given which come from outside of your personal control.

This can be enormously frustrating to an old soul because the old soul is a master controller. When they see gifts from the Supreme coming they appreciate it but then think, 'What can I do to get more of that? How can I make certain this always happens?' The Creator blessedly takes that soul and plays with them the way the Buddha played with his monks.

The only consolation I can offer you for your pain is that on the other side of it, it is as though it never existed. Ascendancy is so simple that you will find it too simple to ever explain, even though many will demand that you explain it. You will find yourself doing the very same cosmic dance with them that we do with you.

Each time you reach the place of true bliss, know it can be forever this time. Keep expecting that this time be forever. If you come out of it, it is only the false pride that then says, "See, one more time you fooled yourself. See how it isn't possible?" If the false ego says that, you don't have to give it any credibility. Sometimes enlightened persons don't speak to others about it because others might tend to say, "Well, that's what you said the last time." The truth is that one time you will forget to come out and it will be forever.

Hearing the Buddha's story made me realize that I was not defective after all. I had felt stupid because it was taking me so long to grasp what the great Masters seemed to achieve so easily. It was reassuring to know that even the Buddha had struggled with the process. Yet, I still felt frustrated. Even though the Buddha went through what I was facing, I still hated feeling this way. I resented the sheer magnitude of the process, not to mention the difficulty of the task. It seemed never to end; there was always more. I clearly had no appreciation for the process. I wanted it done.

There is one thing holding you and that is your very scientific mind. The scientific mind tries to hold on to some sense of objective reality so as not to go on some facile journey into a dimension of illusion and grandeur. That scares you and that keeps you from a final shift. Every form of genius that has come into this world has had to suspend existing notions of reality. Every visionary questions whether they are losing touch with reality and then inevitably must create a reality that supports their perceptions. The only thing that defines sanity is how much collective agreement is available. But that has little to do with what is sane or insane, real or unreal.

Reality is not the point. The point is truth. Perhaps this seems like semantics, but what I mean is that the truth is a living spirit, a life force that is intelligent, unlimited, and capable of change. If there is an ultimate truth about life and truth it would have to be that thought creates itself and it creates reality. It doesn't need to be an individual's thought alone. Group thoughts can also manifest physical reality. Group thoughts can include thoughts of animals, plants, human beings and spirits of all kinds.

There is no point to existence save love. All other powers are there but at best are grains without love. Love is the power that nurtures and gives meaning to every dimension.

CHAPTER 9

AVATAR NATURE

You are fully enlightened but it needs to unfold,
mature, and ripen. You have been born into your enlightenment
and now you have to grow up in it. – Philos

I continued to be absorbed in marathon meditations. I was slowly coming out of one of these long sessions and preparing to drive to Isaac's house for New Year's Eve when suddenly I felt something inside of me crack. My body softened, as if it were melting. Although it was an unusual sensation, I was not the least bit afraid as I found myself swimming in a sensuous sea of love.

As I became part of that amorous liquid, I became so spacious and languid that the boundaries of my body seemed to lose definition. I couldn't tell where I stopped and the air around me began. It was like bathing in waters of ecstasy which were both within me and all around. I was like a fetus floating in warm amniotic fluid, before my body had really taken shape or form.

In this state, I could barely walk, much less drive. I got in the car anyway and drove at 15 mph down a 65 mph four lane highway to Isaac's house. When Isaac saw me he was concerned, but not overly so. This wasn't the first time he had seen me in some altered state of consciousness.

"I don't know exactly what's happening, but it feels incredible and I know it's good," I reassured him. My words were to reassure myself as well. He reached out to hold me in the warmth and safety of his strong arms, which was the most reassuring thing of all. I was dissolving and I didn't know how far it would go. I thought that perhaps my body would dissipate entirely and I'd be released into Spirit.

Throughout the night and into New Year's Day, this delicious dissolution of form continued. It held the promise that I would be tranfigured into something, something special and wonderful. The sensations were so extreme that I couldn't talk, move or interact with the world. I had fleeting thoughts that I might be going crazy, but I also had a very deep feeling of the rightness of what was happening. It was what I had imagined enlightenment would feel like, so I was able to let go. I could do nothing else anyway, as the process was in control. I was not.

After melting for sixteen hours, I began to feel as if a ceiling were opening above my head as something inside of me cracked open. The energies intensified to a fevered pitch and my body began to rock wildly. A deep terror of annihilation rose up in me until I found myself screaming, "I want to go home! I give myself, my whole being over to you. I surrender!"

Suddenly, I felt as if God reached down, grabbed me and pulled me up through the dimensions. A beam of energy pierced my chest and went directly into the heart of my heart, the inner sanctum. A beautiful circle surrounded by tiny diamonds just like my God ring was placed in my heart to symbolize a union, a coming home. I found myself face to face with the Divine, as if I could literally reach out and touch the face of God. Gratitude welled up inside of me and a torrent of tears streamed from my eyes as I recognized my connection to All That Is.

In that moment of grateful surrender I felt memory after memory, identity after identity falling away. I heard myself shout aloud, "I'm free! I've done it! I'm free!" A group of the Ascended Masters came rushing toward me. Among them were Great Chief White Eagle, the Buddha, Yeshua, Philos, Merlin, Miriam, Sun Bear, Astarte, Isis, and Devorah and the Archangel Mikael. They bowed before me, honoring this sacred event. It was a most glorious reunion and celebration as I realized that these were my best friends; I had always been with them.

My mind began to race, "Am I enlightened now?" I turned to Philos, "Is this it? Have I done it?" *You are fully enlightened but it needs to unfold, mature and ripen. You have been born into your enlightenment and now you have to grow up in it.*

Still unable to move, I stayed in the energies. Gradually, the waves flowing through my body slowed down to such a degree that I was released into a state of pure consciousness. At one point, I opened my eyes and looked down toward my legs. My entire physical body seemed to have disappeared and was imperceptible to my eyes.

I was unable to move from this state for five hours. Gradually I felt some tingling around my mouth as the tissue began to revive as if coming out of a deep freeze. I was slowly able to emit some inarticulate sounds and eventually a few words. Then my head began to rock, generating an impulse that moved down my spine and enlivened my extremities. Finally, I was able to stand upright and to gingerly walk again. I felt like a toddler taking my very first steps.

It was soon after this experience that strange phenomena began to occur. The first happened when I attempted to bilocate or reproduce my body and send this double to my friend Kristy's house. I wanted to see if I could ring her doorbell. Seconds after I focused on this, the phone rang and it was Kristy. She frantically told me that she had just walked out of her house to get in her car and that her car was gone.

"Kristy, exactly where was the car parked? Was it near the doorbell?"

"Yes, it was parked directly in front of the door, why?"

"I have a funny feeling that..." Kristy interrupted with a loud yell, "Oh my God, there it is way over in the bushes!" She dropped the phone with a sharp clang and ran out to examine her car. I stayed on the line waiting. She returned breathlessly, "My car is in the bushes lodged between two trees, but so neatly placed that there is not a scratch. How on earth did it get over there?"

"Could it have rolled?" I asked.

"No, the ground is perfectly flat," she replied. "When I parked the car last night, I put on the emergency brake and locked the doors as usual."

"Is there a strong wind, or could someone have pushed it?" I persisted.

"Anamika, what is going on?" she demanded suspiciously.

"Well, Kristy," I began hesitantly, "The only thing I can think of is that I attempted to ring your doorbell and maybe I missed. Sorry."

It was difficult to believe that the energy I had projected over there had been strong enough to move a car, but there was no other explanation that seemed plausible. Later, when I asked the Guides about it they told me that, indeed, my little experiment with bilocation had moved her car. They called it a mechanical response, a law of physics. When you push on a mass with enough force, the mass will move in that direction, they patiently explained. So, if you send enough energy toward a car, it will move the car.

In my attempt to create a facsimile of myself, evidently my energy hit the car instead of the doorbell, and with enough force to move it. This was very hard to believe, but I could find no other explanation for this unusual occurrence.

The second phenomenon occurred during Sakkara. Mataare had joined me to channel the Guides while I was transmitting Sakkara's energies. The Guides were able to explain the function and purpose of the energies, thus adding a wealth of understanding.

As I was recounting the story about moving Kristy's car, just as I got to the part about ringing the doorbell, an actual doorbell began to ring. Stunned, I stopped my story and everyone began to search for the source of the doorbell sound. Mataare, who was not in trance at the moment, jumped up and ran to the door to inspect. Since we were in a hotel conference room there were no doorbells to be found. Clearly, the sound had come from the ethers. We were all amazed.

Several minutes later, the lights first began to flicker and then blink on and off in an odd, irregular pattern. We called the hotel staff to report the problem. They informed us that there was no difficulty with the lights in any other part of the building.

Then, as if this weren't already a strain on my rational mind, Mataare and I went to his house during the lunch break. While he was in the living room gathering some blank tape cassettes, I walked toward the kitchen to prepare lunch. As I rounded the corner into the kitchen there was a huge crash, clatter and bang. I jumped and let out a startled shriek.

Mataare came rushing in to track down the sound. As there was nothing visible, he began to open the cabinets. We found that all of the pots and pans in the cabinet directly across from where I had been standing had come crashing down off their shelves. They were lying in a disorganized heap on the cabinet floor.

When I checked with the Guides about the various phenomena they explained that the doorbell ringing and the lights flickering were orchestrated by them and that the dishes clattering was another mechanical response to my energy. They went on to explain that the reason there appears to be structure to the physical universe is because energy moves. *Electrons travel around the nucleus of an atom at the rate of six miles per second in general. Energy in such fast motion gives the appearance of solidity of structure. When energy quickens and moves faster within one's auric field, as in various states of enlightenment, it increases the speed of that movement and produces effects and phenomena. That very movement is what creates the appearance of physical solidity, as well as light and sound.*

After receiving this explanation from the Guides I was relieved and thought the issue of phenomena was complete. However, I was proven wrong when my favorite black wool sweater mysteriously disappeared. I had taken it along with me one evening in case the temperature dropped. It was casually draped over my arm as I was engaged in conversation with Isaac. While we were speaking, I had noticed it on my arm and literally ten seconds later it was gone!

Isaac and I immediately sprang into action to find the sweater, dashing up and down a steep flight of stairs several times in vain. We questioned everyone in the vicinity as to its whereabouts and came up empty-handed.

Prior to my last conversation with the Guides I would have been certain that I had mysteriously lost the sweater. However, more than likely there is a spirit running around in some dimension who is quite warmly, not to mention elegantly dressed! Unless, of course, it simply dematerialized.

I greatly wanted to understand more about enlightenment. Do phenomena always occur? How does life change? What does one become? I requested of Mataare that he channel the Guides so that I could gain greater perspective. Mataare complied, went into trance and when Philos came through he instantly launched into the story of Yeshua's enlightenment:

There have been many who have awakened into their enlightenment who have left great traditions of misunderstanding behind. Among them is Yeshua. He has since recognized that this occurred because of his ego. He now remains in touch with the people of this dimension to correct the misunderstanding left behind at the time of his awakening and enlightenment. Even though your revelations that come along with this level of awakening are best interpreted and understood by you, it is helpful to hear of the lives of those that have gone before, so I'm sharing his story with you.

Yeshua was a soul who was born enlightened to a very wise and brilliant mother, Miriam. Her father was a rabbi who was glad to have a child for he was quite old and so was his wife Hannah. It did not matter that this child was not the boy he had always wanted. He taught and schooled her from a very young age, passing on everything he knew, which was quite unusual to do for a girl in those times.

Miriam married a much older man. She was hardly fourteen and Yusef was nearly forty. She raised her son Yeshua in the same way she was raised. Because of prophecies that had been given, astrologers and other wise souls came and visited Yeshua. Throughout his younger years they brought Miriam many of their teachings, scrolls and writings which Miriam studied and taught to Yeshua.

Yeshua developed an avid thirst for knowledge. He sought out various teachers and spent years with each one in different places: Persia, Afghanistan, India, China, Tibet, Japan and many places in the Near and Far East.

Upon returning to the land of his birth to teach, Yeshua felt such a sense of mission, power, light and importance that he could not help but be filled with love and a sense of great responsibility. His intent was to teach amongst the Essenes and other Jews. He felt the need to raise the condition of his people and to reach other persons who would be open to him.

Yeshua was the fulfillment of a particular prophecy but he was never recognized. This had to do with the final lesson that every enlightened soul must face before leaving this plane. That lesson is not to save the world.

When Yeshua returned to the land of his birth he had become so learned, so awakened and enlightened, that nobody could understand him or relate to him. So compelling was his sense of mission, that he felt that to reach people he must present himself in a light that demanded others to recognize him. Rather than saying, 'I am the son of man,' he presented himself as the 'Son of God' so that he could get attention and people could benefit by who he was.

The intent was good and many did listen. But what then occurred was that as many drew near to him, he set himself up on a pedestal that further disconnected him from those around him. From his lofty vantage point they could not hear his message that they were as he was. He was seen as special, as above, and as especially gifted. The people saw themselves as unable to understand his teachings and messages of awakening. This very much thwarted his effectiveness.

Yeshua was warned by many other teachers and rabbis to change how he was teaching, but he did not listen. When he was crucified he went into the light and met with the Source. Now remember, he was already enlightened and yet was still capable of making errors along the way and of learning many things. One might say he was further embracing his enlightenment. When in death he met the Source of this existence he was told, 'Go back and undo what you have done.' But in going back into his physical body he found that he could not unravel the zeal of those who had followed him. Yeshua realized that the only way they would ever really understand was to remove himself from their presence. Thus, he told them he would remain with them for a time and then leave.

Some think he actually ascended into the heavens at his crucifixion, but this was more like an extraterrestrial trick. Many extraterrestrials had been watching him as they watch many gifted and enlightened souls. These particular extraterrestrials were the Elohim, and they were seeking to influence humankind for their own ends, and in particular directions which they thought would advance humanity.

Yeshua simply left his followers and continued to travel around the globe teaching from a different perspective and not making himself so important. He traveled all over the world, particularly with the Polynesians who were very good sailors, teaching in a different manner and continuing his learning. Sadly, he could never really unravel what he had begun.

"Was his crucifixion predestined or the result of his actions?" I asked.

Let us say it was a manifestation of his death urge. He believed all along he would die.

"You mean he didn't have to be crucified?" I asked in amazement.

He believed that if he died and came back it would make people listen.

"That wasn't such a wise thing to do." I said judgmentally.

Now you say that rather casually, Anamika, but you forget what it feels like to be filled with that power and light and watch people suffering while knowing that they don't have to. It was compassion that moved him. Nevertheless, it ended up creating in part a tyranny and a great deal of misunderstanding which he is now trying to reteach from the ethers. There is no Master who has ever come into this world who has not faced the very same challenge. Not saving the world is the final test.

It was fascinating to hear of the lives of the Masters from the Guides' perspective. What they shared felt more authentic to me than what had been passed down as historical truth. The Guides loved to teach through story and they were trying to show me that I was not alone in my experiences, but in fact, was following in their tracks. They wanted me to understand that like these Masters, I was an ordinary human.

I loved and respected the Guides so much. They were my anchor in the storm, my sturdy ship in a raging sea. I don't know what I would have done without them. Yet, I was impatient to get it right, to become perfect and forever fixed, so I kept pushing and demanding of them with questions.

"Philos, I understand that enlightenment is an infinite process, but what would you say about reaching full enlightenment? Is there such a thing?"

No, there is not such a thing. There are many beliefs in the world about what enlightenment is and isn't, and the more ideas that you form about it the longer it will take. Part of enlightenment is the recognition or the acceptance of it peacefully. Accept it for yourself and do not let it be challenged by any other source. We do see you embracing all of it and we are quite glad for you. You have touched a deeper, more meaningful communion in your being.

All of this talk about ascendancy, enlightenment and acceptance was wonderful. However, I didn't understand the process of how to get from here to there and my personal life was in a state of unrest.

First, there was my relationship with Isaac. We had a very sweet emotional connection, mutual respect and great comfort. Yet, I did not feel passionate love for him. Our relationship felt more like brother and sister, so my urge for deep intimacy was not satisfied.

Isaac insisted that if we got married we could grow into that deep love with each other. He argued that relationship is a spiritual path and if we made the choice to commit, the passion would grow.

While he had a valid point, I didn't feel that I could marry him on potential. I also didn't feel that any amount of work would take us to the passion I longed for in relationship. Yet, with Isaac I felt secure, and I didn't want to let that go.

I was still having visions and dreams about a man with bright blue eyes who seemed to be my true soul mate. I could not let that image go either. I had to find out if I was crazy or if this man really existed. He felt like the one with whom I wanted to be.

Try as I might, I couldn't let go of that dream. I had a very clear picture of this man, down to the brand of shoes he wore. In fact, every psychic I'd ever consulted described the same exact picture. Didn't that prove he was real?

The Guides had a different perspective. *How do you know that you're not just seeing the way he looked in another life and that the memory is so powerful that it's in your field for everyone to read? How do you know that he looks like that in this life?"* I couldn't answer that. I felt crushed at the possibility that this image wasn't what he really looked like. All I could say for certain is that his image persisted; it would not go away.

I couldn't understand how I could feel him so strongly, as if he were so close and yet he never materialized in the flesh. It was becoming more and more agonizing not to be with him, nor to know if he existed.

Unable to solve this dilemma, I threw my energy into my work life. I held several Sakkaras a week, which were fascinating and profoundly fulfilling. At the same time, Mataare and I were getting closer and closer. Whenever we spent time together our connection would instigate tremendous growth for both of us.

To help us grow in our relationship, the Guides spoke to me directly while addressing Mataare within his own consciousness while he was in trance doing a reading for me. He'd come out of trance with some awareness that something had changed for him, even though he could not specifically say what.

Mataare and I were yin and yang about everything, even about the Guides. I couldn't get enough of them and he couldn't resist them strongly enough. I was wide open to the Guides, trusted them, believed them, listened to them and followed them. They would talk to Mataare and advise him precisely as to what would be of most benefit to him and he'd do the exact opposite. We were continually in a tug of war.

He couldn't believe that I was so open to Sakkara and the Guides and I couldn't believe that he was so closed. To me, it seemed that we had access to some of the clearest guidance possible. In addition, the most spectacular healings would happen when he would let me work on him or he would channel for me. I lived for those moments and he couldn't wait to get away from all of it.

Despite this, Mataare and I grew closer and closer. Our souls were woven together by an invisible thread which compelled us to spend time together. We encountered constant problems personally, yet I couldn't keep away from him.

It was confounding. Equally confounding was that ever since I began absorbing so much love from Mataare, the Guides, Sakkara and Shamuki, I was beginning to experience more and more self-hatred.

Much darkness still lurked beneath the smooth surface. I carried an image of perfection that I tried to embody. If every single detail of life didn't go the way I expected, I would blame myself and conclude that I must be a terrible person. My expectation was that life be seamlessly smooth and graceful, without any challenges. Needless to say, it never was.

Therefore, I felt that life wasn't working because there was some horrendous flaw in me. I was too ugly, too fat, too controlling, too manipulative, too ungrateful, too something or not enough something else. I'd find some reason to beat myself up because nothing ever measured up to my image of perfection. This meant that everything was my fault for which I needed to be punished.

I was faced with example after example of how brutally unforgiving I had been toward myself. I was miles from the gentle self-acceptance and self-love the Guides counseled. Fortunately, I understood that recognizing these patterns was a vital part of the process. I was becoming more proficient at noticing the patterns in action. I would catch myself going over my list of my faults and be able to admit that I was doing it. Then, I'd take a deep breath and recall the words of the Guides:

You are a spirit which is aimed toward your ascension. That is your priority. But there are wounds you have had in the world which necessitate your healing first. Facing these wounds helps you ascend even though the time to heal seems to slow you down. Every time you embrace God, an expansive presence shall come into your heart. Eventually, so many God particles shall collect in your heart that an explosion shall occur that will hold you in the embrace permanently. Then you shall not be able to let go of it.

"They're right," I kept saying to encourage myself onward through these horrible bouts of self-rejection. "Just remember their words."

CHAPTER 10

The Theft

At this point you have no more choices
other than to love me. – God

God took my appointment book. One moment it was with me and the next moment it was gone! I was in my car and had taken it out to check an address, and I know for certain that I put it directly back in my bag. Moments later, I reached into my bag to take it out again and it was gone. I took some momentary solace in the fact that I never lose anything, and retraced my steps. I had only gone from my car to an office, so there weren't that many places to search. I combed them all, but no book!

I sat in my car with my heart pounding, desperately trying to calm down. It's only an appointment book, I reassured myself. However, a hysterical voice in my head reminded me of the numerous times I had told myself that if I ever lost my book, my life would be over. So much for calming down, I was in a full blown panic, "Oh, my God! Where is my book? I couldn't have lost it; I'm too organized for that! Where is my book?"

Then, I remembered that if I calmed down, I might be able to hear an answer to that question from Spirit. I took several deep breaths and waited. An unnervingly steady voice replied: *I have your book, Anamika. I took it from you.*

"What do you mean you have my book? You mean you dematerialized it like my black sweater? Is that you speaking to me God?"

Yes, Anamika, I took your book and I have it.

"I'm going to talk to you through Mataare about this tomorrow!" I threatened.

Very well, came the unruffled reply.

The next day Miriam came through Mataare to speak to me. She told me that it was important that I surrender the book entirely and to trust God to give me everything I needed. She said that it was time to let go of the part of me that was highly organized and linear because I often carried that to an extreme to make myself feel safe. She told me that the loss was actually an opportunity to let go of that fearful part of myself.

Here was a chance to trust in the goodness of God. I wanted my book back, but I also wanted to do the right thing. I wanted to do what was best in God's eyes. I was terrified of doing the wrong thing and consequently became confused. I didn't know whether to try to get my old book back or to go out and buy another one.

"What should I do?" I asked. "How do I know what is the highest path? Should I just go out and buy a new book or just wait to see what happens? I can wait a few days but, I do need to know where I am supposed to be and at what time. Eventually, I'll have to have something to write in."

In the last sixty seconds you have used the word 'should' twice, 'need' once and 'have to' once. Nowhere did we hear, 'This is what I would like to do, wish to do, or want to do.' Your problem is the fear of being judged. Because of this fear you try to stay within the positive aspect of the presumed judgment. This intense sense of judgment is what God is trying to lift from you.

Harmony comes from a place of forgiveness, unconditional love and acceptance. The very confusion that you now experience is the exact experience Creator wants you to have. In the confusion of not knowing what you must do, you will find out that everything is all right. There is no right or wrong, Creator doesn't care. Would you like to speak to Creator now?

"Speak to Creator? Well, uh, yes, I would," I gasped in amazed awe.

The voice of God began to speak through Mataare in a direct, matter-of-fact way, just like I had heard in my head the day before. Unlike the Spirit Guides who had uniquely colorful accents, God sounded almost like Mataare's usual speaking voice but with a distinctly different quality.

Hello Anamika, you've called me here.

I immediately burst into tears. I couldn't believe it! I was talking to God! I could feel the immensity of God's simple, straightforward, intense love. It was absolutely overpowering. Wave after wave of love washed over and through me. Cascades of bliss and rapture rendered me helpless and entranced. All I wanted was to be swallowed alive and never come out.

It was the most astounding contrast; the absolutely prosaic voice of God speaking through Mataare combined with the energy presence of the Divine. This love overshadowed the immense and pure love I had felt from Chief Great White Eagle, Yeshua and the others. I had come to associate Mataare's vocal alterations when he channeled as a necessary aspect of the presence of other dimensions, and now God needed nothing but pure love to communicate. Mataare's voice would do just fine.

I was also shaking from fright. Racked with conflicting feelings, I was torn apart by the magnitude of what I was feeling. I wanted to embrace God through Mataare and at the same time grovel in adoration. I wanted to leap into God's arms and share all of my secrets, knowing that I was safe from all harm. Simultaneously, I feared that I would be judged deficient and relegated to eternal obscurity, punishment, banishment or annihilation. Somehow, I had to prove myself worthy of God's love. The only solution I could see was that I be torn apart cell by cell and remade anew in a better form.

You're crying. You don't have to be afraid of me Anamika, but if you wish to be, I'll embrace it. I'm here to help you join me, to be in your highest self. As you seek to do that, it is important that you don't invalidate the part of yourself that you are leaving behind. I come to you to expand the ways that I can be with you. Ask of me only what you feel is really important.

I racked my brains to see what was really important because I still wanted to do it right. My first impulse was to ask about my appointment book, but I quickly censored that thought. As much as it worried me, I couldn't very well qualify that as *really important.*

I realized that there wasn't anything at all practical that would satisfy that requirement. Nothing mattered but the feeling of God's love. With this realization, I dropped out of my mind, down into my heart and sought the real question. After a moment, something came to me. Still afraid of being wrong, I tentatively ventured, "God, how can I love you more?"

I don't think you can love me more. You love me with all of your being and I feel it. What stops you from feeling more love is that there are parts of yourself you haven't discovered how to love yet. My angels and spirits will teach you how to love those parts of yourself. I can't teach you those things because I am you. I love your love and I draw you into me with all of my being. You can't resist who I am. Isn't that beautiful?

The love radiating from God was so exquisitely compelling that I felt helplessly drawn in. I didn't want it ever to end. This was the great love I had been seeking, the one that touched my innermost yearning. This love was not only everything that I thought I would experience with the ideal soul mate, it was more, much, much more.

At this point you have no more choices other than to love me. There are experiences that human beings have where they deny themselves. That is not acceptable to me. If I cannot show you how to change that, then I shall send the angels and saints in the physical and non-physical dimensions of the world so that you can be taught how to accept all parts of yourself. I also send you one of my Lords, Yeshua, who is here with me now so that we can speak like this.

Bathed in this much love, my fear stood out in stark relief. All of my parts were indeed exposed and obvious. I was embarrassed and ashamed of myself, not at all accepting of all of my parts as God had urged.

Still, I was beginning to feel bolder, so I asked for more. "God, I have so much fear and judgment. Can you help me with this?"

Anamika, I've already accepted that. All of your fear and judgment I love. I take that from you even now. Where you do not know how to do this, I will help you. That's why I snatched your book away from you. Get another book if you want to, but you can't have that one back until I'm ready. Is this pleasing to you?

Strangely enough, it was pleasing. I had a glimpse of the freedom that would be available if my attachment to the book could be broken. It was light and liberating and I felt like laughing. I also felt an unexpected pleasure that I wasn't in control. For someone who thrives on being in control, I was surprised by the abundant joy of such surrender. What a relief to not have to do everything myself. I didn't have to be in charge of my life. There was a God that was wiser than I. I replied, "In some strange way, yes that gives me pleasure. I truly don't know what I really want."

Many make that mistake. What you want is confused with things you don't want. You had to throw out what you did want just to get rid of what you didn't want. Then, you judged what you do want as unimportant. Now, I want to give you what you want. Will you receive this from me? You must have the courage to know what you want. Do not be afraid to make mistakes, or to walk into territory that seems to be dangerous to you. Have faith in me.

As God said this, a realization washed over me. I was utterly afraid of doing things wrong. Making mistakes was a form of death in my mind. I attempted to focus on what I would ask for if I weren't afraid of being imperfect. Nothing came. If being imperfect was okay, I was stumped. With nothing to lose, I asked the question that I had judged too imperfect to ask, "Can you tell me why you took the book?"

Yes. It was making you suffer by tying you to the world and keeping you from looking toward me. I don't want anything between you and me.

I was stunned! This was absolutely the last motivation I would have imagined and the antithesis of what I had assumed. I could not have had a more glaring example of how little I knew of God and of my own limited perspective. I had thought I was being punished. Actually, I had built a testament to my fear and ignorance and God had taken it away from me.

God's desire for our closeness thrilled me no end! I felt myself sigh from the relief of understanding God's book robbery. God's desire for closeness and mine were the same. I offered back, "I don't want anything between us either."

Do you know that I love you now or do you feel judged?

"I know that you are loving me."

That's good, Anamika, because I am.

"I am also feeling confused right now, and speechless."

I come to you in this way deliberately to confuse your picture of me and to open your being to what I really am. You would like to see me in a grandiose way, but I want to come to you closer than that. That's how you need me so that's how I come.

"You almost seem a little stern."

I'm sorry. That's the part that you feel judged by. You must learn to see through that to who I really am. I'm not stern at all, I'm just direct. I directly love you.

"Right now I feel a deep fear of being judged, though I know you are helping me with this. I also feel that if I don't do it right you will take your love away. I fear that you are going to leave before I ever really find you."

It felt so good to be able to admit these deep fears. It was as if a great stone were being lifted off of me. I now felt weightless by comparison. My breath seemed to become energized and light as I spoke of these dark concerns that I had withheld even from myself.

I do have eternal unconditional love, but I don't have infinite power. I don't have the power to take my love away from you. There is no way you can instruct me how to do that. It's not within my ability. This is something you are able to do because you have never known the kind of love that I have. Once you know this kind of love you will see it's impossible for it to ever go away.

"I'm afraid that I am unworthy of you."

Why are you afraid you are unworthy of me? How good do you have to be?

"I don't feel that who I am is good enough."

I understand that's why you think you have to be someone else, have to do this, have to do that, need to do this and should do that. Anamika, I love you completely, always and forever. It's impossible for me to feel anything else for you.

I love you when you're clear; I love you when you're unclear. I love you when you're doubtful; I love you when you have faith. I love you when you're high; I love you when you're silly. I love you when I give you things; I love you when I take things away. I love you always and eternally without limit, without end, and beyond your knowing.

I place my love in certain ones around you who are able to love you the way I am able to. You are worthy. If you don't feel worthy, I will keep sending you angels, teachers, signs and all of that boring stuff that I have to wait for you to get through so that I can finally have you in the way that I want. Would you like me to send you some angels, teachers, signs and all of those things?

I loved the angels and guides. It shocked me that God thought this was boring. On the other hand, I did want God as purely as possible. "No, I would rather just have a direct relationship with you."

Excellent, but I want you to know that I will send all of those things too if you want them. Those things are wonderful, but it's tiresome for me waiting for you. I ache to have you with me completely.

God aching? Now I was shocked and thrilled even more. I didn't know God had such feelings. I had no idea that God's feelings were the same as mine! I knew that I had been aching all of my life! Had God been aching throughout all of eternity? If so, I wanted to ease God's ache, but I didn't know how.

Just believe me. Claim that you are worthy. Your disbelief will surface, but decide it's worth more to you to believe me than not. I don't want you to believe in me, I want you to know me. Believe that you are worthy, and that will teach you to know me. Only through your belief in your worthiness can you then know me. Your belief in your unworthiness will prevent you from knowing me.

God was saying I needed to believe in myself. My lack of self-worth was not humility, it was self-judgment. That judgment had kept me separate from God and in great pain. Real humility was my openness to God's love and the acceptance of our union. I had always felt so alone that it was difficult to admit that I needed God's love. I had taken such pride in my independence, continually reinforcing the illusion of separation.

This illusion created greater and greater suffering. So, like an addict, I perpetually reached outside of myself for something to ease the pain, something like my long-awaited soul mate.

I don't know why you made up that idea of soul mate. I know soul mate exists for you in the way that you look at life and things. It exists for many in your world. I want to give you something far beyond what you can imagine. Will you also let me do that?

"Yes, of course!" I was elated at this prospect!

Thank you. And my angels, saints, and guides will see to your soul mate business. They will help you with that but I will give you something more. Do you love me now, Anamika?

I was overwhelmed with love. "Yes, with all of my heart and soul."

I love you now. I love you forever. I love you in your spirit and I love you in your body. I love you in your soul and I love you in your being. I love you in all parts of yourself. It makes us happy that you love us, that you love me. Can you stand me this personal with you?

I had to admit that I was squirming from the discomfort that this level of personal intimacy produced, even though it was what I most desired.

When I leave, you will long for me. I will answer your longing in many ways. Look for me in many ways and you'll be able to receive me more when I come to you directly again and again in personal and impersonal forms. I want you to recognize me any way that I am. You don't need to fear that you will or won't be able to do that. You must remember that I am the Supreme Instructor and I will find ways to teach you. Will you have faith in me in that way?

"I will, God."

I love you.

As God departed I felt myself reaching to hold on. I didn't want God to leave. Just as God had predicted, I instantly felt a desperate longing to be together again. Then suddenly Mataare's voice began to speak again. It was still God!

I never really left, Anamika. I knew you wanted to hear my voice again, so here I am. I'll come every time you want, not always in the form you are expecting, but I will always come every single time you want.

"That's what I want." I heaved a huge sigh of relief.

We'll see how true that is. Talk to me regularly within your being. I have given you free will with the privilege of separating from me if you choose and the privilege of joining me if you choose. Both are good. Now I want something from you. I want your devotion and I want your undying love. This is what I want from you. I want all of it and I want it now.

As I heard these words, my hesitancy disappeared. All I wanted to do was to open up every cell and fiber of my being in ecstatic mergence. I wanted to join permanently with this profound and ultimate love which was now available to me. I wanted to hold back nothing. Never before had I felt this degree of unconditional desire in which every single part of me was screaming, "Yes, now!"

Taking a deep breath, I began to pour my heart out to God. Big round tears welled up and spilled down my cheeks. God felt my love and responded.

Thank you. Now you are receiving mine.

I felt God's love pouring into me, filling me up. By now I was crying from deep gratitude and blessed love.

Now you understand, beloved. Blessings.

God disappeared suddenly. I was startled by the abrupt departure, but did not feel the loss and sadness I had earlier when I thought God had left. This time I felt so filled, so whole and so indescribably wonderful that there was no room for emptiness.

I realized I could let go of the book and when I got a new one, I would not recreate the old one. I would record only what I needed now, nothing from the past. It seemed fitting that the new book reflect my new awareness and perspective. Breaking the attachment to the old left me free as never before.

Later that day, Mataare called sounding very upbeat and chipper. When I asked him why he sounded so cheery he said that he was finally getting organized. He had gone out earlier in the day and bought an appointment book so he could keep track of everything. Before I could get a word in, he started raving about what an impressive book he'd gotten; it had so many sections, it was such a nice maroon color, and it was so well organized. It turned out to be the exact same brand, color, and style of book as the one that had been taken from me! "You have my book!" I exclaimed.

It wasn't just that Mataare had gotten an appointment book, it was that had he had gotten the specific one that had been taken from me. God's lesson showed up here with graphic clarity. I needed to be freer, spontaneous, and less rigidly organized. Mataare needed to learn focus and organization. It made perfect sense that he now had the book.

I laughed at the cosmic irony of it, and the clever, subtle way that God works. The experiences of love for me and for Mataare were precisely tailored to what we each most needed. I had given up something I thought I'd die without and, not only had I lived, I felt better than ever! I breathed a sigh of relief. How easy it turned out to be and how gloriously wonderful God was!

Actually, if I had known then that this was only the beginning of what I'd have to give up... but I didn't know that then. I naively and blissfully thought I had done my giving up and letting go.

Soon after this incident, while I was speaking with Constance through Mataare, the undeniable presence of God showed up again. Just as God had predicted, I had longed for this connection incessantly and was therefore thrilled to speak to God in this way again.

I am with you Anamika. We come to you and you come to us so that we can be together. I come simply to be with you.

"Oh, good," I swooned. "That's what I want more than anything in the world. I didn't think you'd ever come back again. I'm ecstatic that you're here and I want to tell you that I love you so much." Spontaneously, tears began to rise from my belly and spill over.

Anamika, I love you. I love you so much.

"Good, I want all of you."

How much of me do you want?

"All of you. I want the whole thing." I began laughing.

Oh, you make me so happy, my Anamika. You are such a joy to me. Tell me that again. God crowed in a delighted, childlike tone.

"I want all of you. More than you can ever imagine."

Oh, my Anamika, you just made your God so happy!

"I want every ounce of you."

Oh yes, and I'll give you everything that you are able to handle and more. You need to be able to embrace the love that I have for you because if I give you too much it won't always seem like love. Tell me again, how much do you want?

God was having fun playing our little game. "I want it all." I was having fun playing this game too, because it felt good to want it, to ask for it, and to know that it might be given.

Oh, how wonderful. We are going to have a lot of talks. I want you to talk with me more often inside of your being and I'll be very easy to access. I am leaving this form now.

"Can you come to me in this way when I need you?"

Yes, because I love you and because you love me. If I don't come in this form it's also because I love you. A true holy, sacred relationship is one in which the love becomes more important than some sort of construct or form that you think you want to make yourself feel safe and secure.

God departed suddenly, leaving me wondering. Constance picked up where God left off:

People think that that's what relationships are for. While they do give some security, safety, and some healing sometimes, the purpose of a relationship is for you to go far beyond those things. Your soul requires that you find your truth in God. If your truth is in God and you experience God in your relationship then you can get your security in the God in your relationship. But certainly the relationship can't replace God for you. You cannot use a relationship as your God.

Many people try to do this only to break up resentfully years later full of hatred for each other, because they tried to make themselves what the other one wanted. It's just so ridiculous when you can just go ahead and love each other totally as you are now, without trying to make each other into anything. But it doesn't mean it's going to be the relationship that you want. It will be the relationship that it is. The realization is: 'We're going to have to love each other the way we are or not at all and whether or not it meets our conditions.'

That certainly is love that is unconditional. Quite a tall order, I mused.

CHAPTER 11

Ascension Day

When you know yourself as Source, you have total understanding that you are not threatened by the minuscule encounters which can seem so big. – Miriam

I had fallen head over heels in love with God. Our conversations were the most satisfying and purest moments of my life. I wished for every moment to be as these. At the same time my relationship with Mataare had strengthened and he more frequently joined me in Sakkara. During one such Sakkara in Sarasota, Florida, the Guides discussed the process of ascension and awakening.

Fully awakened beings, or Avatars, are keenly aware that they are both infinite and finite. They never forget that they are infinite and a source of the miraculous in the world. They also never forget that they are finite. Therefore, when they encounter signs of their humanity, they are untroubled by it; the judgment goes away. An Avatar continually confirms, affirms and recognizes that she is totally supported by the universe.

When you know yourself as Source, you have total understanding that you are not threatened by the minuscule encounters which can seem so big. Even if you did see yourself as threatened you would laugh and say, 'Oh, look at my finite self feeling threatened by this,' and it would be instantly released. There would not be fear attached for very long if at all. You would be able to cope with it as well as be able to instantly transmute it into some other form of usable energy to you.

Ascension means the lessening of the period of time needed to transmute energy into something that is a lesson or an advanced condition. As you get better and better at doing this, the time spent in struggle shrinks until every single experience of love or confrontation is experienced exactly the same way. It is welcomed as an opportunity to transmute it or use it for something which benefits you, without going through struggle to get to that point.

Then, you would see that your challenges happen specifically to give you the opportunity to go into your bliss again. You would say, 'God is so precious. God just

gave me another opportunity to be in my bliss. Thank you.' It will become habitual for you to use everything to feel your bliss or to acknowledge when you don't, and then open to feeling it.

Again and again the Masters had reiterated that I was in the ascension process, yet I doubted their word because I had an image of ascension as an unchanging state of bliss and divine light. I certainly wasn't in any such state. While I did experience otherworldly energies quite often, I was continually cycling through emotional highs and lows in a very human fashion. Therefore, I continuously questioned why I wasn't feeling constant rapture. I had erroneously concluded that ascension meant vibrating at a higher state of consciousness and embodying a different reality, one of static and constant joy.

The Guides explained that indeed the ascension process was a change of frequency. It was an awakening to the experience that we are one with the fabric of the universe, which is God or love. However, every Master, no matter how awakened, experiences ups and downs, highs and lows. No one stays in a peak experience at all times they informed me. Because the Masters articulated their peak experiences, many people have erroneously assumed that the Masters were in those peak states all of the time.

When I was with the Guides, I felt whole, joyous and expansive. But, I didn't feel this way all the time in my daily life. They understood me and what I was experiencing, which I so desperately needed. While I had many friends, it was only the Guides who could truly touch me where it mattered. When I was not with them I felt cold and inconsolably alone.

All who seek to take a step into their ascended nature at some point have the sense of doing so quite alone. You must not fear that aloneness. It is the embrace of the void, and the void is just as important as the light. You have danced with the void and danced with the light in preparation for this movement. This dance is not complete; it goes on forever. You are learning how to become so intimate with this dance with the void and the light so as to know that you are bonded forever in the joy of the Godhead.

It is very important for you to be in divine communion with yourself and the divinity that is intercoursing with your spirit. This divinity must become your constant and eternal friend. It stands with you in every instance and expression so that you see yourself as one with God. This shall require no new or particular focus on your part, simply a willingness to be completely yourself. In that relaxed selfness you will see how all things make sense and how you are supported by the light.

As I was preparing to leave Sarasota after an illuminating Sakkara about awakening and ascension, I had a vision of a little white stucco beach cottage.

It was beautiful, set on a crystalline white sand beach with an orchard of fruit trees and tropical flowers surrounding it. The tingling I experienced throughout my body indicated that this was where I was to live. The vision was so clear and blissful that I didn't even question that I would be leaving behind the life it took me twenty years to build. I just knew I would do it.

Later, on the plane, I was in a deep meditative state with my eyes closed when I felt the presence of someone before me. I looked up and there was Yeshua gazing at me intently. It struck me like a thunderbolt; Yeshua is my Master Teacher!

Yeshua smiled warmly. *You are being prepared to connect with my Master Teacher. Are you ready?* I knew that Yeshua's Master Teacher was God and I excitedly nodded that I was ready. *Very well then, tomorrow is the day.* He bent over and kissed me tenderly on the forehead and then on the lips. I glanced down at my calendar, which happened to be open in my lap. In small print it said, "Ascension Day."

I awoke on Ascension Day with a great sense of anticipation. Yeshua had said that because so many people are focused on the image of Christ ascending on this day, a window of opportunity is opened. When Yeshua had said that today was the day, I wasn't sure what he had meant. Did he mean that some ascension would occur today? Was this the day when my life would change forever? I would be leading a Sakkara later in the day and perhaps a miracle would occur there I hoped.

A large crowd was gathered for the Sakkara and I noticed a special electricity in the air. As I breathed deeply and allowed the energy transmission to move through me, I saw a sizeable etheric window opening in the center of the room. I heard Miriam say: *It is most important that you come to this window of ascension with a pure heart and a clear intention. It is the strength of your intention that shall allow you to pass through the window that is now opening.*

Others had noticed the window as well, and we all moved into the opening together. Each person began to experience his or her own version of the ascension process. In the sacred silence, I heard God speak to me inside of my being. *Are you ready to embrace Me more completely?*

"Yes, I am," I responded earnestly.

God flooded the room with love saying: *I have always been here. I never left. It is you who has experienced the separation to explore aspects of your being. You have been crying out for love from a place of deep agony within your soul for many years and you have not heard me. I have been here in the faces and voices of all of those around you and yet you have not seen or heard Me. I have received your rage and your anguish as well as your love. It has been you who has needed to receive me.*

The truth of this perspective struck me like a jackhammer and I again realized that God was in as deep an agony as I was. I vowed to remember to consider God's point of view as well as my own from now on.

I was overcome with the need to apologize for my rejecting ways. It was indeed me pushing away, and then rejecting and blaming God for rejecting me. In a flash I saw how my yearning for a soul mate was really a desire for union with the Divine. I had been looking for a person to fill the hole, to give me the feeling of the union instead of opening to the Source within on a personal, intimate level.

I am in your every day life in the most ordinary and mundane ways, which is why I speak to you in your own voice. Understand that you are an aspect of me. Be yourself completely. Know that you are worthy. You are me. Do you question my worth? Then how can you question your worth? You must come to know who you are. You are love itself, the very fabric of all of existence.

Suddenly, a shell of my identity as I had known myself cracked and fell off. I soared through ecstasy, bliss, peace and freedom and was elevated into the eternal embrace once again. Then BOOM, I was thrust right back into my body. A veil of perceived separation had dissolved.

God's voice spoke again. *Welcome home, Anamika.*

I was stunned by the utter simplicity yet profundity of these words. There was a crystalline clarity as if I were truly in the present moment for the first time in my life. Everything was contained in the here and now and in my body. I had no sense of past or future, here or there, inside or outside, up or down, back or front. It was all the same, all right here, right now. I laughed at this cosmic joke that I had worked for billions of years to get to where I had been all along, right here, right now. In fact, there was nowhere to go. I realized that ascension was awakening to the truth that already existed. I could feel that the very cells of my being were divine love itself, love incarnate.

I looked back over the many stages it took to get to this place. There had been poignancy, sacredness, yearning, endless hours of devotion, pleas, prayers, tears, rage at the heavens, fears of opening, constant surrender and consistent faith. When it was all said and done, it was so anticlimactic, so matter of fact, and yet so profound. The drama that I had anticipated would accompany this moment was also an illusion, a misconception about the true nature of life.

"Oh, life is just life," I laughed, "and I am who I am and so be it."

CHAPTER 12

MERLIN'S MAGIC

Fear not for anything whether you are antagonized
by persons or circumstances. This is all simply the completion
of necessary karmas that free you to embrace yourself
on the highest level. – Merlin

My vision of moving to Florida was quickly becoming a reality. Unmistakable signs leading to this change had begun and I couldn't help feeling unsettled. Although I knew that this move was the next step, it was an enormous change as I would be leaving behind my entire life, including Isaac.

For some time now Isaac and I had been moving in different directions. As I had been drawn more deeply into the spiritual path, I was becoming less of the world. This pleased me as I was responding to the dictates of my own awakening.

Isaac, on the other hand, was becoming more and more involved in earthly things, thinking most particularly about restaurants and movies, which were of no interest to me. Yet, as much as I felt ready to end the relationship, I also enjoyed being with him. We shared a certain comfort and safety that was not easy to relinquish.

At the same time that I was pulling away from Isaac, Mataare and I were growing closer. We were increasingly magnetized to each other. We were able to feel God directly through each other, even when he wasn't channeling the Guides. Needless to say, being able to feel God directly in any way certainly got my attention and I craved spending time with Mataare.

I spoke to Mataare about all of this. Just like me, he was both excited and frightened by the prospect of becoming closer. As I lived in Massachusetts and he lived in Florida, we spent most of our time talking and deeply communing on the phone. Responding to messages from the Guides, we decided to take a trip to Mexico together. Mataare flew to Boston for the preparation.

Excited about our upcoming adventure, we stopped at a local stationary store to buy a map of Mexico. I waited in the car while Mataare jumped out in search of the map. When Mataare came back to the car he told me that he had been unable to find one. He was about to leave the store empty-handed when Merlin jumped into his body, found the map, paid for it and then popped back out of his body. I was getting used to this by now. "Thanks, Merlin," I said aloud into the air.

When we arrived back at my house, Mataare and I were sitting at the kitchen table drinking tea and pouring over the map when Merlin again decided it was time for a visit and popped back into Mataare's body. Since I was somewhat used to Merlin usurping Mataare's consciousness, I was able to continue our discussion with minimal adjustment.

We were deep in conversation about Mexico when a realtor and her clients showed up at the kitchen door. My house was now for sale in preparation for the move to Florida, and the people who arrived had come to view it. I looked at Merlin and asked telepathically, "Are you staying or leaving? If you were Mataare at this moment, I know you would behave. But given the prankster that you are, I don't trust you not to make trouble." He gave me a knowing wink, so I swallowed hard, praying that this outlandish situation wouldn't blow a potential sale.

I opened the door for the people and introduced myself. I didn't introduce Merlin - how exactly would I introduce him anyway? Ignoring my pleas, he piped up anyway in his inimitable English accent, making some small talk. The visitors didn't seem to notice anything amiss as Merlin was acting rather casual and relaxed. Since he wasn't creating any mischief, I figured that perhaps he could charm them or even encourage the sale of the house. The visitors left without incident and Merlin gave me another knowing wink. Eventually, as fate would have it, these were the people who did buy the house.

The trip to the Yucatan in Mexico was magical. Together, Mataare and I followed clues left by birds and animals to ancient ruins and followed an itinerary outlined by the Guides. Mataare and I were not lovers, and I still didn't think he would become my one and only true soul mate. However, the charge was building and we bonded deeply during this trip. Every minute together was stimulating, adventurous and exciting.

On our return trip, Mataare and I jumped onto an earlier flight than the one for which we had originally been scheduled. The flight began smoothly enough but we soon encountered horrendous turbulence. As I was reaching for the vomit bag in the seat pocket in front of me, I heard Merlin's distinctive voice, *Hello, Anamika, are you not feeling well?*

I looked over at Mataare, and sure enough, there was Merlin in Mataare's body. He snatched the bag from me and stuffed it back in the seat pocket. *I don't think that will be necessary. We had you booked on the later flight to avoid this turbulence, but since you are here...*

Merlin spread out his arms like airplane wings, took a deep breath and then closed his eyes to increase his focus and concentration. Within seconds the plane began to stabilize. My stomach relaxed.

"That was a great trick, Merlin. I appreciate the help, believe me. I'll have to try it myself sometime," I said. On the next leg of the flight we hit more turbulence and I tried the trick. Sure enough, Merlin's magic worked.

As I began to let go of my career, my life in Massachusetts and the security of my relationship with Isaac, Mataare joined me in more and more Sakkaras. It was a wonderful blessing as well as a natural blend of our energies. Being together in this way was heaven on earth for both of us.

Over time, the energies became so intense between us that it was virtually impossible to stay away from each other. Not only did the tension have to break, but also we needed to express the electricity and passion of our romance of the soul. Simply touching each other took us both directly into God and opened our energy systems so completely that we couldn't find words. Entwined for hours we journeyed through doorway after doorway after doorway into dimensions previously unknown.

While I was soaring in my relationship with Mataare, I felt wrenching conflict about Isaac and battering guilt about the many inelegant ways I was handling the separation. I was terrified about my upcoming move. It was so frightening for me to leave that I made a rather large mistake. I had wanted to end my relationship with Isaac gracefully and with integrity. Instead, I betrayed him by sleeping with Mataare. One day, we finally made love. Being with Mataare in this way was beyond anything either one of us had experienced. One could barely label it a sexual experience because it went so far beyond anything we could put in that category.

I had never betrayed anyone like that before and was mortified at my own behavior. In fact, I felt so terrible, that I couldn't forgive myself. Looking for relief and clear perspective, I broached this sore subject with the Guides after a Sakkara.

Merlin had generously stayed in Mataare's body expressly so that I could speak with him. He turned to me and whispered that I should stay seated with him until everyone had left because he wanted to have a few words with me. He knew I was plagued with guilt. I was relieved to speak with him, but terrified he would blame me as I was blaming myself for engaging too soon with Mataare and betraying Isaac.

"I can't understand what happened, I just felt compelled to be with Mataare. I felt no control over my actions. I am terrified because I have betrayed Isaac even after promising that I would always be honest with him."

Part of it was your fear, but we pushed you and Mataare because we were trying to stir up issues for all three of you and give you enough help to get all of you to work through your issues.

Mataare and I were very open, sensitive and impressionable and at the time felt confused that the Guides had pushed us like that. I felt the rightness of being with Mataare, but I wished I had ended things cleanly with Isaac first. It was only later that I both remembered that I had given the Guides carte blanche to move my life forward and also later came to see the wisdom of their actions. In the end I was grateful but I had a lot to work through to arrive at that point.

I was caught in extreme terror about moving, leaving, and having my whole life uprooted. On the outside I acted as if I were fine, but on the inside I was out of my mind and totally irrational as old emotional patterns surfaced. The terror that had come up when I lost my appointment book paled in comparison to this. Letting go of my entire life as I had known it was utterly overwhelming, yet, I knew I wanted to do it. Still, I was horrified and humiliated to see my fears create such a mess. I had always prided myself on my self-control and integrity. So much for my pride! Here I was swamped in the sewer eating humble pie again and again.

To make matters worse, I knew Mataare and I would not be in a romantic relationship for long. Our personalities were too opposite, so that even though on a spiritual level we were totally one, we could never make it together long term. It would just be too stressful on a personal level. We didn't really have the ability to talk things through sufficiently. I couldn't accept where he was coming from and he could not accept my point of view. We were like the proverbial oil and water; we just didn't mix.

"Oh, Merlin, I feel like I'm doing a very poor job during this transition time. I'm falling into terror of letting go and therefore not completing with Isaac as quickly and easily as I think I should. I'm terrified because I'm leaving Isaac and terrified that I've betrayed him as we are shifting our relationship. I'm making a huge mess! When I'm this fearful I loose sight of the big picture that everything is all right. Then, I really feel unsafe."

Yes, because you do not know yourself on these levels you are now exploring. This is where the part of your being, which people need to know and cannot know, gets discovered. You are, in fact, doing a rather superb job at allowing yourself to explore this dimension of your being. If it takes more time than you intended it to take, so be it.

Isaac is forcing you to look at your greatest fears: fear of loss, fear of attack, fear of being burned alive, persecuted, blamed and sentenced for mistakes that you are making. He is also blaming you for things that are not your responsibility but are his projections.

"I keep blaming myself with thoughts like, 'If only I could do it better then I would have figured out how to have a true partner by now.' Or, 'I should be perfect enough to never make mistakes or hurt anyone. I'm stupid, bad, weak and wrong and it's all my fault.'"

Ah, beloved, you are in very good company. You are not alone with that inability to draw in true partnership. Have you not realized that spiritually awakened beings are with partners quite different than they are? Hasn't that ever made you wonder? It isn't that you are doing anything wrong. Also, everyone makes mistakes.

There is a great challenge that lies ahead of you that shall not always be easy. Fear not for anything whether you are antagonized by persons or circumstances. This is all simply the completion of necessary karmas that free you to embrace yourself on the highest level. It shall draw from you that which you were not aware of possessing and lead you to find the miracle of light and power that you truly are, the miracle of Love and wisdom that you truly are, and the miracle of the oracle that you truly are. This is not a path of ease you have chosen but it shall not exhaust you; it shall develop and nurture you and reveal to you the truth about existence.

I feel very much like your friend today. Perhaps we shall be seeing a great deal of each other. I think you might become the best friend I have in this world, Anamika. We have a great deal in common.

I was so moved by Merlin befriending me in such a personal way that the gut-wrenching knot in my stomach finally relaxed. Framing the situation as part of my soul's lessons helped me feel more at peace about the triangle with Mataare and Isaac and about my impending move. Now, if I could only hold that peace until the day I was scheduled to drive away from my old life and into my new one, I might be able to breathe.

CHAPTER 13

THE GREAT DELUSION

You must end seeking to find a place that is without flaws. Instead, find that place of forgiveness and surrender. – Miriam

Once I had committed to the move, many synchronous events occurred. Since I had seen the vision of the crystal sands in Sarasota, I knew that that was where I would be going. My parents had just moved to Sarasota and my mother gave me the name of her realtor. One morning I felt the Guides pressing me to call the realtor now, NOW! They insisted that I pick up the phone immediately and call, so I did. I described my vision of the white beach cottage and said that it had to be a place that would take a dog. She replied, "I'm sorry, I have nothing like that. That's going to be really difficult to find and besides, most places don't take dogs."

Just at that moment, a woman walked into the real estate office and announced that her beach cottage had just become available and that pets were okay. The realtor described the property to me. It matched my vision to the detail. "That's it!" I said, "I'll take it."

I sold my house and furniture. What I couldn't sell, I gave away. The only things Shamuki and I kept to take with us were his bowls, leash, toothbrush and flea comb, and my computer, car and a few personal items. Everything else was gone.

It all happened so quickly. No sooner had I firmly decided that I would follow my vision than the world as I had constructed it began to unravel. It was as if everything was arranged to move me forward.

Before I knew it, the day of the move arrived. The sky was overcast and light drizzle was falling. The grayness reflected my inner mood exactly. I had chosen this path even though I had no idea what this move would bring. Leaving everything behind was not as easy as I naively thought it would be. It hurt.

I had packed the car and my house was empty. I took one last walk around the yard, remembering how this home had sheltered Shamuki and me for so many years. Now, I was letting it go so that it could hold someone else while I went to a place I had only seen in a vision.

Isaac was waiting by the car to drive to Florida with me. I felt a deep pain that I was also letting go of him as well as my friends, community, work, income and the area in which I had lived for twenty-two years. I felt overwhelmed with sadness and wanted to collapse on the damp ground and cry forever. Shamuki nudged my hand, acknowledging my grief and urging me to leave. There would be time to cry later.

After several uneventful days on the road, we arrived at the beach cottage. It was as beautiful as the vision and newly renovated with fresh white stucco. The vaulted ceilings offered ample space for the colorful stained glass windows that looked out on a magnificent two million dollar estate. A plush green lawn rolled down to a private, crystalline white sand beach, which fronted the sparkling aqua ocean. The trees were laden with figs, oranges, grapefruits, limes, lemons, and bananas. There was every kind of tropical flower you can imagine and then some. A wooden footbridge spanned a pond filled with plump well-fed coy fish. An artistically sculpted asymmetrical swimming pool completed the scene. What a romantic tropical paradise!

The cottage provided a cozy nest. It was quite small but pristine and lovely. As it was already furnished with floral prints and rattan, there was nothing I needed. I set up my computer, positioned Shamuki's bowls, hung up his leash and my clothes, and that was that. I was ready to go, but where?

Isaac stayed for several days, providing a welcome delay to letting go of our relationship. Putting him on the plane back to Boston was one of the hardest things I ever had to do. It was final, our relationship was over. The separation was something I had wanted and yet had been so afraid to face.

As soon as he was out of sight I felt utterly and inconsolably alone. I walked out of the airport in a haze of grief to find my parked car. I fumbled for my keys and managed to climb into the car before the floodgates sprung open. It was as if the deepest wound in my soul tore apart and I fell into the dark abyss of the void. I understood for the first time why people feel they cannot or will not make it through. It was all I could do to take the next breath as I wailed and screamed to God, "Please help me survive, help me make it through this transition!"

For weeks, I spent eight to ten hours each day sobbing, begging for help to take the next step. The grief and the terror brought up by letting go of my life in Boston were utter and complete. They became my whole world. I could see why people reach for alcohol or drugs to numb the pain just to survive.

But, I had come too far for that and had to rely on Shamuki and God; I needed large doses of both of them.

Day after day, I sat on the cool, tiled floor of my cottage with a box of tissues and cried my heart out. Shamuki would come over and minister to me. He would lick me, put his paw on my heart, nuzzle in, put his paws around my shoulders and hug me.

Sometimes he would just sit across the room and look at me. Often he would sigh, put his head down on his paws and look up periodically letting me know he was there. He patiently waited for me to move through the pain, never letting me out of his sight. He attended to me constantly no matter whether he was sleeping or awake. Sometimes he'd say, "Okay, let's go outside, that's enough pain for now." He'd drag me out with him to walk on the beach. He made me move my body, even when I didn't want to and I did feel better after walking a bit.

Several weeks passed in this way. I gave myself permission to face all feelings that arose, no matter how painful. Shamuki and I covered every inch of the sparkling beach backwards and forwards many, many times. Playful dolphins came into the cove to befriend us. The pelicans and egrets watched from a nearby wooden pier until Shamuki lunged into the surf and scared them away. Despite the beauty of nature and of these gentle beings, I still felt desolate, alone and inconsolable.

Mataare was the one person I wanted to reach for, but it seemed that the Guides had purposely been keeping us apart. He was continuously on the road working while I was in the deepest agony of the soul. We had seen each other only once briefly during this time. Our love making was exquisite as always, but every time he attempted to go into trance the Guides would pull away. Finally, on my birthday, I was granted a reading and Miriam came through.

Your emptiness doesn't know how to fulfill itself. It keeps trying to take charge of your life in a way that doesn't work. You need to give up control and allow Creator, in the Creator's time, to give it to you. This teaches you surrender and it is through surrender that all the gifts come. It is not easy until you surrender.

"I feel a lot of pain right now," I sobbed.

You must end seeking to find a place that is without flaws. Instead, find that place of forgiveness and surrender. This is the lesson you are embracing now. This is what we speak of as the final lesson that ends suffering. It is not to say that there are no more lessons or challenges after this. It does not mean that you are perfect after this.

This is baffling and confusing since through lifetime after lifetime you have been wounded over and over in this deepest area of your being. This is why you cannot be responsible for making yourself better. The only thing you can be responsible for is acknowledging when you are in the lesson and for the willingness to turn it into the hands of the Creator.

"Do we just constantly learn lessons? Are you learning lessons too?"

Indeed we are still learning lessons, and so is the Creator of this very existence. Otherwise, we could not be infinite beings. The moment we stop and become unteachable, we are finite.

"Then why do I have this notion that I have to achieve a state of perfection?"

It is the greatest delusion that human beings hold, and it masquerades as spirituality. It is a way to protect the ego and reinforce it, not a way to embrace it and move beyond it. It is a byproduct of the culture and the tendency of humankind.

This tendency is to find the greatest way to survive against all odds. It is a severe and strong survival instinct built into the way life has evolved on this planet. Species and cultures have not found what is truly the highest order, an inter-cooperative rather than a competitive system. In this system, the idea of perfection is not flexible. It is rigidly competitive and thereby doomed to extinction. Only that which is capable of change and flexibility is adaptable enough to be universal and lasting.

Instinctively, you think making mistakes can mean the end of your existence. That is what you have been taught. That is what humankind is taught, but the higher wisdom is beyond the perfection seeking. Have room for forgiveness. This is the only way that souls can know that they are lovable. If they think they must be flawless, they think that they cannot be loved. If souls recognize that forgiveness is a great part of unconditional love then, and only then, can they understand why they are loved.

How right she was. Even though I knew better intellectually, I still had the feeling that I needed to be perfect to be loved. I drove myself incessantly to perform everything correctly, instantly and impeccably.

Those who realize that they can be loved with all their flaws allow themselves to be loved in this way. Otherwise, souls will look for flawless beings or for beings who they believe have achieved a certain high state, and they will not see the God in all. They will never find the one who has achieved that high state without also seeking and finding many flaws. This separates them from the very love they want. This lesson is one you are amidst and will be the primary reason you are able to embrace soul mate. You will no longer be looking for the false image of perfection.

You are still looking for a right and a wrong. You think that if you are right you will be given a present and if you are wrong you will be punished. This is the very paradigm that is creating the problem, the need to be right and the fear of being wrong. The feelings of fear you are having right now must be turned over to God. Let go of this into God and know that you must do this over and over. It is not once and for all, Anamika; it is again and again.

"I feel sick in my soul right now," I moaned.

You are at a choice point. Do you wish to go on in the safety of what you know, or take a risk and surrender to God as you know God within your being? Will you allow the Creator to design your path for you through life lessons? This is the choice that you are facing and that's why you feel sick.

You will feel an absolute desire to recoil into the safety of the known and you may do that if you so choose. You may be convinced that that is right. Don't let me convince you of the rightness of what I say. I am simply here to share with you what I have done that has brought me into this union. You are here in your sincerity, letting yourself receive from me the benefit of my experience in trust. Only you decide that you are willing or able to trust.

The sickness in you wants to hear other things. The sickness in you wants you to do things in alignment with the sickness that produces the same result again and again. You are not the sickness in you. You do not realize that this is the desperation which gets hold of you and controls what you do. You must acknowledge the desperation in order to relinquish it. If you don't, it will grab hold of you and you will end up feeling powerless and destroyed. Instead, you must recognize your ally is the Supreme and must continually resort to that ally.

This is a great opportunity for you to experience breaking through and forgiving yourself. Forgive yourself for not being what you set for yourself to be and forgive yourself for setting that ideal in the first place. This forgiveness needs to be there, for only when that truly happens does one's judgment of others end, as well as the fear of judgment from others. Then, your sickness in the soul will leave.

As a belated birthday surprise, Mataare called me to say he would be joining me for Sakkara in Orlando. After we had gathered in a group Mataare went into trance. I was elated when I recognized that it was God who was present through Mataare. No matter how much I adored each of the Guides, I loved being in the presence of God more than anything in the world. God began to address the group about our human perspectives versus God's point of view:

Maybe what you have been taught to believe is different than the Truth. Everyone screams to the Heavens, 'God where are you?' Did it ever occur to you that I have always been here and that from my point of view I ask, 'Where are you?' Does my perspective surprise you?'

"Yes, it does," a voice from the group piped up.

I have a different orientation to say the least. You can become concerned about things that don't matter to me because of how you've been hurt. The reason you've been hurt is that you are not me. You don't need to become me, you need to love me. I'm not saying you don't love me, I'm saying that to heal, you'll need to love me.

There are two things that get my attention: 'I love you,' and 'Thank you.' Don't forget about those things. You have many concerns. I know this because the helpers tell me all the time. If you want to get my attention directly, 'I love you' and 'thank you' get my attention best.

I turned to God and said, "I want to be with you all the time."

I see that, I feel that, and I hear that a lot. But I don't understand the perception that there is a separation. When people say that, I don't exactly know what they are talking about. If they are talking about something other than the truth that we are together now, I don't understand.

And about that concept of time, it's not about time. When you're with me, you're with me. That's it. There will be lots of moments like that and everything in between doesn't exist. Soon, that will be true for you. When that is true, it won't be all the time. It will just be.

The only way to approach me is from love. Your hurt may create desperation that may inspire you in some way, but you'll need to give it up. The approach will then be from love. Gradually you'll remember love more than you'll remember hurt. The love will heal the hurt.

Your desperation creates an aspiration, which gets you to climb out of the places that you got into. Sometimes you need that. But the aspiration will also get in the way. Just love. Love me. Love anything. Love more. That's what heals the hurt, the separation and the time issue.

There was a pause as everyone was absorbing God's words. Then someone asked, "God, what do we mean to you?"

God sighed with obvious pleasure at this question, and then spoke with deep emotion. *You are my devotion, you are my heart, you are the reason that I exist. You are everything to me. There is nothing that means more to me than you. I exist because of you, for you and through you. There is nothing else.*

There was a long pause. Tears were running down God's cheeks as well as our own. The voice of God had ceased, but God's palpable and powerfully loving presence still permeated the room. We sat suspended in this lingering presence for a very long time.

CHAPTER 14

UNDOING

When there is nothing more to hold onto and you
have found complete faith and safety in the presence
of the Creator, that is the source of the tranquility.
As long as anything remains from which
you draw security there is more to be undone. – Sun Bear

I was living in a tropical paradise by the sea and yet I was depressed, even despite the words from the Guides and God. I had surrendered my career, Isaac, my house and my community. I had thought that letting go of so much would make my life better. I had released so many burdens and had nothing to bind me. "I should be happy," I admonished myself. Yet my heart was breaking from loneliness and despair.

I found myself going deeper and deeper into the hole in the soul, the place where I felt utterly alone and empty. Each day I thought I had gotten through the worst and that it would be getting better now. Yet the next day I felt even more lost, more alone, more desperate and terrified. I had never before had the courage to fully face the bottomless pit within me and acknowledge its depths. I had never faced how utterly terrified I was simply to be alive. I had been covering up this fearful place inside with overwork and distractions. Now I had no distractions; no lover, no friends, no community and even Mataare had pulled away from me.

Thank goodness I had Shamuki. He would slow down to walk at my pace if he felt I was particularly vulnerable that day. Sometimes he would try to get me out of myself by pointing out things in nature or trying to engage me in swimming or playing. When I went through crying jags, which was still quite often, he would press up against me and comfort me with endless patience.

No matter what the situation, Shamuki tried to give me perspective, healing, companionship and love. He was compassionate beyond belief and lived in the state of being in which I yearned to be.

He kept gently encouraging me to come and meet him there. As he was deeply at peace with life and himself, he clearly had attained mastery and was a living example of unlimited and unconditional love.

When Shamuki met people on our walks, he would light up and open himself to communicate deeply with them. Astounded, I would watch him because I would feel myself contracting at the presence of another human while Shamuki expanded. The contrast was stark. I got to see how frightened I was of just existing, of being human. On the surface, anyone meeting me would say I was an outgoing, open and communicative person. While that was true to an extent, what I shielded from them was an inner landscape of icy terror.

I think that it was really a fear of being deeply loved, known and intimate while simultaneously feeling the yearning to be loved, known and merged. My fear was that if I opened myself to be loved that deeply, I'd lose myself and be trapped or judged. Thus, I needed to gird myself and hold tightly to my individuality. However, in so doing I closed to love. I repeatedly seesawed back and forth between open merging and constricted self-protection.

I couldn't seem to find the balance where I could both know myself as me and as one with All. I both yearned for and was afraid of love that was so intimate and personal that I would be cherished and adored in every fiber of my being. What I longed for most I was rejecting and this was also the source of my deepest agony. Ultimately, I didn't understand that this was the human dilemma.

I suppose I had hoped that Mataare would fill the void, or that I would be somehow rewarded for this risky move. This was not the case. What I did get to experience was more of me, and certainly not my favorite parts. The Guides helped me to understand the process.

You came into this world to serve as a teacher of God. Part of your journey includes the experience of having everything of this world removed. Many who are in such a position feel that this is too rigorous. Yet, there is a purpose to it. There is a need to absolutely depend upon the Creator in all things as a resource, realizing humbly that everything comes from the Source. It is only in this way that true security, true fulfillment and true learning can take place for a teacher of God.

In the stage after this, there will come a place of real and true peace. For here, heaven's state is fully reflected. From that point on, the way is open and in some ways easy. From peace you can go anywhere. You will find that tranquility becomes the essence of what your search is for and nothing else shall be placed before that. It will grow more powerful. Look for the peace and tranquility in all that you do. It becomes the search and the find. It is already beginning in you, but cannot be fully present until everything is undone.

"There's more to be undone?" Like a flip chart, my mind rapidly reviewed all that I had let go of already. "What more is there yet to undo?" I asked horrified.

Yes, there is more. When there is nothing more to hold onto and you have found complete faith and safety in the presence of the Creator, that is the source of the tranquility. As long as anything remains from which you draw security there is more to be undone. And only Source knows which things need to be taken.

Each day you must say, 'The highest will be done, not mine.' This allows the Creator to remove from you that which needs to be removed. Any place in your being where you feel a tightening or a need, meet this with the prayer, 'I allow this to be surrendered into the Creator and whatsoever it is that comes, so be it.'

Gradually, following the advice of the Guides, I began to notice that in fact I was changing. Some days were filled with peace and gentle breezes while others were still rugged, rigorous and painful. On the whole, I could tell that the deep fear that I had been facing was actually being transcended.

The pockets of gentle peace I would encounter periodically were extremely soothing to my weary soul. They were the kind of sweet, joyous peace about which I had dreamt. I would have moments and sometimes even hours of feeling in harmony with life, with myself and with the world. In those moments, there was no fear and all was well in my world. I could actually be present with no agenda, needing only to breathe, be alive and in love with that experience.

As I began to feel more moments of appreciation for life without gripping, consuming, gut wrenching terror, I could breathe deeply without yearning to be somewhere else. In peace, there was no need to be touched, met or filled by something outside myself. Life was full in the moment and not a reaction to something external. I was at peace for no particular reason. It was just because I was alive and existed as me.

These tranquil moments would pass and I'd be back in another crying jag, terrified, hysterical, despairing and miserable. Then I'd go for a walk and a bird would fly overhead. I'd feel its beauty and then instantly be at peace once again. The next moment a wave would lap over my feet and I'd dissolve in tears of loss.

The waves of life were moving me, washing over and through me. I was so raw and cracked open that I felt every little nuance of life. It was like being completely out of control and at the whim of whatever was happening with no ability to alter my course. All I could do was show up for the next moment and keep breathing. I had no ability to make choices, decisions or to think about what I would like to do. I had no life other than feeling whatever I was feeling in the moment. I could do nothing but yield to its fancy.

I had left behind the external reflections that had confirmed the identity I had called myself. Instead I was experiencing life as a free flow of emotions and sensations. This way of living was radically different than the tightly controlled life I had lived before. In fact, I began to lose confidence in any sense of self as I gave up control. I even began to lose my perspective about who I was.

When I had an opportunity to speak to the Guides again I told them that I felt I had lost touch with my gifts and my purpose. I asked if they could articulate my gift. Sun Bear came to address me:

Your gifts are two things primarily: 1) the ability to cause spontaneous shifts of consciousness with energy and, 2) your faith, which is much stronger than your beliefs. Faith is what people function on when they don't believe anymore. Faith is that which drives a being when everything else is gone. Because you have so much faith you create spontaneous breakthroughs and miracles around you and in the lives of others. Your faith is huge.

Sometimes faith felt to me like gambling everything on nothing. But in my deepest heart, I knew that faith was really gambling everything on what only appeared to be nothing. It was really gambling nothing on accessing more of everything!

The world is shifting rapidly from third dimensional into fourth dimensional reality. Spirit has come close to this plane giving everybody who wants it the opportunity to make this shift in consciousness. Nobody understands the magnitude of what is happening. What is being done is so immense that the only way it can be done is a miracle that nobody has yet grasped. The only way it can be embraced is by recognizing that it is way beyond you and therefore totally dependent each moment on the grace of the Great Spirit. This is what all of those who have crossed have found in common, that you wake up each day and say, 'I can do this again.' Listen, Anamika, would you like to go through what you have just been through again?

The mere thought was beyond horrifying. Certainly, I would never survive it.

This is why we are pleading with you to just do what is there for today. You can relax; you are doing wonderfully.

"I am?" I asked with great amazement. After each conversation with the Guides I felt clear and uplifted until I looked again at my life.

There, I still felt not only separate from the world, but also separate from the very few people to whom I was close and somehow I thought it should be different.

One major source of comfort and support to me had always been my mother. I was grateful she lived in Sarasota too. However, I no longer felt that the people around me, including my mother, could understand my life. Increasingly, I was living in some other reality. The more I progressed, the more difficulty I was having relating to others.

My mother reflected many of the negative judgments I had about myself. She expected me to get over it already. "What's the problem? You're the one who let go of Isaac. Why are you so miserable? He wanted to marry you and you could have done that and then you'd be living with him. Why are you not getting over this and getting on with your life?"

Being around her would stimulate my own self-judgment and I'd feel desperate to pull myself together and get moving. I'd fall back into thinking that the solution to my situation was an exercise of will that ignored the profound feelings that were part of my transformation. I couldn't exercise my will anymore and she didn't understand the spiritual dimensions that were opening in me. I was being pulled through veils into other dimensions of reality.

Although I tried to explain my experiences to her, it quickly became obvious that I couldn't describe my journey in a way she would understand. In the higher dimensions of existence everything looked differently. The principles were not the same ones as prevailed on Earth. In the higher dimensions were limitless love, compassion, harmony, ease and peace. I would touch into that reality and then be thrust back into the fear-based reality in which most of the world lived.

The longer I dwelled in the new place, the less I could reach back across the dimensions to communicate where I was in a way that anyone, not just my mother, could understand. There was no one around me having the same experiences of ego dissolution and the stripping of karmas. The only ones with whom I could talk were the Guides. Even Mataare and I couldn't really communicate.

Mataare had become furious with me and proceeded to shut me out on a personal level. At the time I couldn't see how I was hurting him. I could only see that he was hurt beyond all measure, and that his stonewalling actions felt abusive and agonizing to me. Fortunately, he could still channel for me. He was amazed by this and repeatedly remarked, "I don't understand how I'm still channeling for you. Normally when a relationship goes this way I can't channel anymore."

Unlike Isaac, Mataare never outwardly blamed me for our situation. He took more ownership for his part as I did for mine. We were both being as honest as we could, but there was no longer an openness between us. We were both too hurt. My heart was broken that I didn't have him close in my life anymore. Other than Shamuki, Mataare was the closest being to my soul. To top things off, he got involved with another woman. I was frightened to death of losing the Guides which I feared could happen because of the state of our relationship. The Guides were my lifeline and it felt like I was hanging on by a thread.

The Guides had told me that even the most spiritually awakened people on the planet could still have things go terribly wrong, or at least seem to go terribly wrong. An awakened person, they explained, would be able to let go of things that go wrong without comparing or judging. This was an enormous lesson as I still wanted everything to be fairy tale perfect.

CHAPTER 15

THE KISS OF GOD

Keep giving your heart despite the pain. Let it tear
and break. This opens more space for love.
It will mend whole. – God

I dreamt that I was in a place I did not recognize, filled with people I did not know. I walked among them, reaching out attempting to connect with someone, but no one seemed to notice me. Then, I saw Isaac at the edge of the crowd and ran to him. I touched his arm, "Oh, Isaac, thank goodness it's you! I was feeling so alone, I'm so glad you're here!"

Isaac turned and looked at me with no recognition in his eyes. He shrugged his arm out of my grasp and walked away. Terrified, I ran, pushing through the crowd until I came to a large mirror. I stopped and looked at the person in the mirror with horror. I didn't know this person. Thinking that perhaps this was a trick, I raised my arm and watched the mirror image as I moved. I spoke and watched the lips in the mirror form words. I screamed, shattering the mirror and falling to the ground in a heap, sobbing and sobbing.

My sobbing woke me. I lay still, looking around at the white walls dappled in sunlight. I recognized the bedspread, so I must have put my things here. Where was I? Who was I? My name... what was my name? As hard as I tried, I could not remember my name. Frantically, I reached for the phone and pushed the redial button, knowing that it would connect me with someone I knew. The phone was answered by a deep male voice I recognized as Isaac.

"Isaac... Do you know who this is?" I asked timidly.

"Is this a trick?" he asked skeptically, colored by his distrust of the changes I'd been through.

"No, please," I begged. "I can't remember who I am. What is my name?"

He heard the desperation in my voice and gently replied, "Anamika. Your name is Anamika."

The sound of my name shot through me with a jolt and I remembered who I was.

Gradually, I began to venture farther from my cottage. Sarasota was a budding spiritual town with health food restaurants, gem shops and arts and crafts stores. Many people in Sarasota were seaching for something new, searching for the light. Shamuki and I would take little forays into town and occassionally stop at the bookstore or the juice bar.

During the course of these excursions I began to meet a few people who seemed interested in my work, so I decided to offer Sakkara. One Sakkara turned into more, and soon I was holding several Sakkaras a week. The size of the group constantly grew and my parents attended every one. Still I had trouble connecting with anyone outside of Sakkara. I was fine when I was in the group, letting the energies flow through me, but I was unable to connect on a personal level with anyone.

One day I got a phone call from Christopher, a man who regularly attended Sakkara. "Anamika, it's time for you to be with people again," he said.

"How impudent!" I thought. This man has no idea what I'm going through. However, a voice inside told me that he did know. I sensed that the voice of God was speaking through Christopher and I knew that he was right. Still, I felt raw and messy and incapable of even having a coherent personal conversation.

A few days later, Christopher called again. This time I heard Yeshua's voice speaking through him. "Let me accompany you for a walk on the beach."

I consented. When we got together I was pleasantly surprised to discover how comfortable and easy it was to be with him. He didn't expect me to talk or tell him anything about my life. He simply walked with me and Shamuki. It felt good to have another human being with us and after he left, I felt better. I had found a potential friend and it made me feel that I would eventually be able to pull myself out of the pit that was engulfing me and gradually join the world again.

Mataare came to Sarasota to join me in Sakkara. Our relationship had become strained and difficult, yet I still looked so forward to seeing him and working with him again. The work we did together was still powerful as we still went to a place so complete, inspiring and full. Truly ours was a divine connection. Yet, on a personal level, we just could not see eye to eye. Mataare didn't stay long; he just came to do the work and then immediately bolted. Still, being with him gave me a boost as always.

Sometime after Mataare's visit I was relieved and grateful to notice that I had begun to feel more connected, both spiritually and physically. In fact, the God energy had begun to break through with such a gentle, compelling force that my whole being felt ignited with divine love. I felt as if I were connected to the very heartbeat of God. This love filled me with a golden light that became white then colorless as the presence of Source radiated out forever and ever.

These experiences were happening more and more often and I was able to sustain them for longer periods of time. I asked Yeshua how to hold onto this feeling. I had worked so hard to find it, I couldn't bear the thought of losing it. He told me to focus on something greater than myself. As I did, I began to feel that I was dissolving. My old identity was falling away at an extremely rapid pace. I had no thoughts, no desire to do anything, no place I wished to go. For days on end, my full attention was absorbed by this unusual dissolution.

The sun came up, burned hot with tropical intensity, and went down. The full moon echoed haunting ancient tribal rhythms. I lay in the sun, my body pulsing with its caress. My skin breathed, moving and merging with the rays of the sun. I slept and awoke, my body unceasingly undulating with waves of divine love.

Throughout this period I could hardly stand upright because the energy coursing through my body was so potent. However, I could dance. There, alone in my cottage, I danced and danced. The movement of the dance which began primal and wild evolved into refined, elegant, flowing undulations. Time had no meaning. Everything was now. I kept letting go, letting go, letting go; there was nothing I wanted to hold. I was a vast ocean, a sea of life with passion bursting from my chest.

"God I love you, I love you. There's nothing but you!" I exulted as wave after wave of exquisite love poured forth from my heart. My soul was singing its song. I was gently drawn into the arms of God. The most tender, caressing hands pierced through the ethers and came toward me. They stroked my face then ran down the length of my body. I heard God speaking to me softly: *You are my lover, my beloved.*

God inhaled and I felt myself physically pulled forward into God's breath. Then God exhaled, breathing energy and life into me through my mouth. The breath of God filled my whole being, creating me anew.

Then God kissed me on the mouth saying, *I want all of you with Me. Will you be wholly mine forever?*

"Yes, I am yours." I melted further and further.

My breath became the fire of life. Each breath became a spark that ignited into a burning white-hot flame that danced throughout my body until I was ablaze.

"God, help me to love you more and more. There is nothing real but this love."

Then I remembered something Yeshua had told me, *You must know what you are, not only who you are.* "I know now!" I thought. "I am radiant brilliant light. No matter what my personal issues are, they are so minor, so incidental compared to the brilliant radiant light that I am!"

For several weeks I floated in this new knowledge of what and who I am. Then, I began turning back toward the dark side of the moon. Ascension Day was approaching and the darkness inside of me was intensifying. There was a full eclipse of the sun that matched my feelings. I felt like a puppet. One minute I would be radiantly happy and ecstatic and then for no apparent reason, I would shift into a mood of dark, bleak despair.

As the time of the eclipse approached, I could feel enormous pressure building inside me. I realized how powerfully I was influenced by not just the moon, but by the movements of all of the planets, the galaxy and the collective energies. When there was an event like an eclipse came, it would sweep over me like a tidal wave and I would have to yield. I didn't have a choice; it was stronger than I was.

I was wedged between the pain brought up by the eclipse and the promise held by Ascension Day. The eclipse tore my heart apart and brought more unresolved wounds to the surface. For twenty-four hours I was thrust back into a place of separation. I felt no hope of ever feeling love again. The darkness closed in and I wanted to die. Where there had been love there was now only sadness. Where was the woman who had danced in ecstatic frenzy? That memory seemed like that of another life.

I turned inside for answers. For every light side, there is darkness. For every darkness there is light. "Help me find the light again," I prayed. I heard the voice of God. *Keep giving your heart despite the pain. Let it tear and break. This opens more space for love. It will mend whole.*

"I have nothing left to give you, God. I am broken down, lost in the ruins of my shattered heart. Help me let go and remember your embrace. Help me know you dwell in me even here, in this darkest recess of the bottomless black hole."

Nothing changed that day. I had planned a wonderful gathering of people to celebrate this day of ascension, yet at the beginning of event, awaiting the presence of Sakkara I felt lost, hopeless and alone. As we all joined in and spoke our intention for the evening, I heard my uninspired voice say, "I wish to enter the colorless God ray once again and to stay there this time." I had no real hope of this happening, but I asked for everything anyway.

The drums began. Soon, the geometric forms of Sakkara and the Ascended Masters entered the room. I was so numb and dull that I did not feel connected to Sakkara's energies at all. My only recourse was to let go into my breath and physical movement.

I breathed deeply and stood up. As the drumbeat intensified and my movement increased, the numbness began to melt. Rage arose within me, a wild, primal animal rage. Quickly this rage became so intense that my body could barely contain the energy coursing through it. I found myself in a primitive, tribal frenzy, as if in a trance possessed by Spirit.

My arms waved about wildly, my muscles filled and pumped with raw animal power. My long, thick, black curls flew with abandon and the power of the energy flung me onto the floor in a writhing inarticulate heap. The power was so intense that all I could hear were silent screams of rage at God for all of my pain and for all of the world's pain. Rage poured out of each cell and filled my breath. The next thing I knew, I was collapsed on the floor.

As I was vibrating with so much energy, I defiantly scrambled back onto my feet shouting, "I hate you, God! I hate you, God! I hate you!"

It occurred to me for a brief moment that the participants might think I was crazy, but this thought was quickly overwhelmed by the all-consuming feelings. This dance of rage sustained at a wild pitch for over an hour. I had no idea that my body could endure such prolonged frenzied movement.

One by one others joined me until everyone was thrashing about as wildly as I was. As we continued, our passion became more and more inflamed. Each moment seemed to be the height of a fevered pitch. We couldn't imagine a more intense degree of consuming heat. However, just as any given moment's intensity surpassed the last, it too gave way to the next moment's inferno.

The energies grew even stronger, as if someone had turned up the volume of a spiritual amplifier and the room became electrified and charged. My inner voice burst forth in a silent scream that shattered the fabric of our fury. "That's it! I will take no more pain! I have had enough of this subjugation! I hereby claim my God consciousness! I am free to be completely and entirely my full self! I am myself!"

Millennia of women's oppression and denial of our strength stormed through me. I would not stand for it. I would not stand for reaching for God outside myself. I would not stand for any renunciation of myself. I knew that I was beautiful and complete right now. I claimed myself as I had never done before.

As I did so a thrashing tumultuous bolt of actual lightening materialized, flashed and exploded in the very center of the room. It scattered bodies right and left with its force then disappeared just as our frenzy came to its consummation. As it turned from yellow into blue and then white gold, we were thrown in exhausted heaps back onto the floor. Time stood still as we experienced the great void that is the opening to God's space.

I lifted my eyes to see the spot where the lightening had struck. Through the thinning mist I saw an etheric, rectangular frame hovering in the air. Inside its perimeter was another veil. It was as if the veil that had obscured my vision of God had become visible.

I knew that I was being given a clear choice. I could to enter into God's love or remain in perpetual inconsequentiality. Without a conscious effort or choice, I expanded my awareness so that I could accept this geometric invitation to step through the window into the next phase of my destiny.

I arose, flew across the room and stepped through the frame. On the other side of the veil there was only white light. This light beckoned and invited me to merge with it so that we would become one. The sensation was that of all consuming love. At last, I was there with God again. The colorless God presence of exquisite, unnamable love poured through my being and I was home again.

This time I did not need to ask whether this was my ascendant nature. I knew, beyond all doubt, that it was. I fell deeply into love. I looked around the room to see what was occurring for the other people. They were profoundly touched by this palpable love. It infused everyone for a time before it gently subsided so that we could communicate and relate in a more everyday human fashion, but we chose not to. No one wished to disturb the sacred fabric of our experience as we sat there speechless in silent communion with each other.

Gradually we broke away, holding the Oneness within ourselves. As everyone slowly left to go home, I needed to stay close to someone who had experienced this extraordinary evening. I invited Christopher, my sweet new friend, to come back to my cottage with me for a while. Christopher, Shamuki and I walked on the white sand beach under the new moon and bright stars while reveling in the warm tropical breeze. We wrapped our arms around each other, our feet in the gentle waves. The three of us stood in a sacred embrace, surrendered to the same Source, all three knowing we were that Source, each seeing God in the others.

We sat on the beach in this magical mood all night. Christopher left early in the morning and I finally laid down to welcome sleep. When I awoke a few hours later, it was a bright, clear morning. I could still feel the divine love coursing through my body. It was Ascension Day.

CHAPTER 16

DARK ANGEL

Within each person is an untapped, immaculate, and indescribable power which is the guiding intelligence at work throughout all existence. – Yeshua

Ascension Day arrived and I was elated to be having a reading with the Guides. Happily, it was Yeshua who came through to talk to me on this special day.

Within each person is an untapped, immaculate, and indescribable power which is the guiding intelligence at work throughout all existence. It is untapped until the time when one is entirely embraced by it because of their surrender. This force is so beautiful and so powerful that merely by its residence within, one benefits. Eventually, it intertwines itself in all of one's affairs.

When one becomes aware of this inner resource, the search begins to tap it. As the journey is embarked upon there comes a powerful unfolding that time and time again reveals beauty, even when one lives in the outer perimeter of its beingness. This Source requires everything to truly be known.

I came to see my primary purpose as to pass on a message, a truth, to help others to embrace that truth and to reveal the truth as I had come to understand it, to those who would have an ear to hear. Increasingly, my desire to convey this message and the desire of the people of this world to receive it did not match. This surprised me, but eventually I came to understand that just because a thing was of the truth as I saw it, it did not mean that others would embrace it. I felt all alone.

In my aloneness I sought a friend and I entertained that counsel. I hoped it would gratify and give to me the fulfillment and validation I needed. The counsel I came to know is what you would call the ego and which I called the Dark Angel. This did give me the validation I sought, but with each validation I had no idea it was the ego, the shadow self, which I had to entirely release. It was a self which I did not understand and which would pursue me my entire existence in this world. I later came to understand it and I ceased to battle, for I found the meaning of true surrender and I let go.

The lessons I learned were harsh and difficult. I confused this harsh Dark Angel, or shadow self, with the Source. Later I came to find what it means to truly seek the Truth. The point where I came to understand that is what you would call ascension.

Through the seeking of my Source and the unwitting counsel of the Dark Angel in my loneliness and in my purpose, I realized I could not do this alone. So, I gathered to me those who would support my mission and purpose and who were dedicated to the same purpose. I never called them my disciples, they called themselves that. I simply gathered those I thought had the same purpose as me. The best they could understand was an entity that existed as God in a Heaven. Some had one God and some had many.

Although they could not believe what I believed, they could believe that I believed. This brought grace to them and they came to know a greater God in what I described. They had faith in me, and I beckoned them to have faith in me. Such was my certainty, for I knew they would find their blessings through their faith in me, for I knew I already had salvation, at least in my beliefs. Yet I still felt alone.

Surrounding me was tremendous power, grace and light. There was much that I did not understand even though I believed I did. This I found to be so when I was crucified, tortured unto death and then did rise. This suffering was a great sacrifice which I had learned and been taught to make. Those who were my teachers spoke to me of sacrifice, to sacrifice myself to the Source of this existence in utter abandon and then perhaps I would be received by others.

I practiced this with my teachers and I was aware there would be a greater sacrifice to come. I felt that if I were to make a supreme sacrifice then those who would come after me would not have to sacrifice anything and could then focus upon love.

I cannot hope that anyone would fully understand the rationale behind this because it came to me as a revelation and I understood it. It was not for anyone else. It was for me and was a part of my journey, so I went in that direction, understanding the best that I could understand.

All the while my Dark Angel persisted and it plagued, hounded and tortured me. It created the loneliness and went right alongside with the powerful revelation I had prior to my ascension. The Dark Angel would beckon to me amidst my greatest joy and sometimes my deepest pain. Sometimes I could not tell the difference.

Since I believed that I was here to sacrifice myself, I believed that my deepest pain was supposed to exist, it became part of my spirituality. I thus did not think that something was wrong since I believed I was supposed to suffer, and that my suffering was part of a greater good. Since I believed this, but it was not so in truth, from time to time I questioned my God, my understanding, and I simply could not understand completely. What I could not understand I chose not to think of.

This was made clear to me at one point, for I had a great, great discovery. This was perhaps the first of several powerful discoveries. I had a vision that came in the time of my dying. In that vision I was told by God to go back to the world and undo what I had done. This was a tremendous shock and a tremendous freedom. It was the beginning of my liberation and the beginning of the end of my loneliness.

You shall find visions that shall come in some of the ways that I did. The native people of the North American continent showed me how to induce these visions by a three-day juice fast. Then, I climbed into a hole in the Earth, which was five feet deep and four feet wide with nothing but a blanket for five days. I stayed there with no food or water until the ants, crickets and other bugs became my teachers. I was in prayer and meditation, having such visions. There shall come a time when you shall do something similar.

In the time of my ascension, this vision was induced for I did come unto death. When I returned from this experience, it was a confusing time for me, for I had to change my ways completely and I did not know how. All of my life prior to that time had led me to believe a certain way and now I didn't know what to do or believe.

What I saw was that I had to leave behind the dearest people to me, those who called themselves my disciples. I knew they would prosper in my absence and yet I feared the loneliness again. I had passed on to them the teachings I had learned from all of the Masters. I had given to them as I was so freely given to. I gave away everything I had learned and I came to the end of that journey. I could not pass on any more.

I did not know the meaning of undoing what I had done, not then. I had been asked to give up everything when I thought that I already had given up everything. I realized that I had to move on and that my disciples would also have to move on one day. Unlike the way that I had done it, moving on from teacher to teacher, these ones did not know to move on from me.

I had told them to hold onto me because I did not believe they could do or would do as I had done all over the world. I did not believe they could make the sacrifices I had made. I later came to see that I did not trust that they could find their way. Instead, I told them to depend upon me. This was a part of my Dark Angel because I saw myself as their salvation. I realized that they, unlike me, could not move on because I had instructed them not to by telling them things like, 'But through me there is no way to the Kingdom.'

If you are true to that which is within you, the unlimited and powerful force that is the guiding intelligence, then you will be guided by the Spirit that is there. Ascension requires true humility. It comes from putting yourself in the guidance of other teachers. After I left my disciples I did continue my work and I did travel the world. From time to time I came to great Masters and humbled myself before them and learned from them. They also received from me. I did not try to have them understand the greatness that I did come to know within myself, for I realized that if I wanted to learn from them I had to be like everyone else, small and receiving.

These Masters helped end my loneliness. They were the teachers who were sent to me by this indescribable resource that is perfect in its guidance and intelligence. But this Teacher teaches only the humble and requires everything. That which is not humble will not and cannot find this Teacher. This Teacher requires absolutely scrupulous honesty. This is something that is sought and perhaps never fully found. There are always aspects of one's character, even my own as I exist here in spirit, that contain many imperfections.

The way I became humble was to continue to surrender myself no matter how the teacher would appear. They could come in the greatest or smallest ways. I put myself in their guidance and said, "Show me this way. I need to learn." In this way, a part of me remained small that had previously grown large. The Dark Angel no longer ruled me. I could recognize this shadow self when it did appear and I was no longer lonely because of that recognition. I no longer listened to it, and recognized the things in myself that were my dangers. Mine were grandiosity and fear. There were others I did carry and they never did disappear. They were with me my entire life, but I came to accept these and did not mind.

When there was pain that I did not understand I knew that the trouble was me, not the world or any the external circumstances. I knew there were parts within myself that I needed to yield in order to embrace this unnamable and unlimited resource which required something of me to hear its whispering voice.

My awakening to this and the acceptance of all parts of myself was my true ascension. From this realization day forward I was free, happy, and truly joyous. There were still trials from time to time and life for me was like life for everyone else. There were good days and bad days, and sometimes I wished my family would disappear and sometimes I was happy with them.

The one thing that never happened for me anymore was the deepest part of the pain that was brought by the Dark Angel, by the parts of myself which could never be perfect. These things in me I had learned to find acceptance for and did find serenity. Then, every single day was a good one in my mind not based upon achievement or the knowledge that every day is good, but because I truly and deeply appreciated this unnamable resource which I had become one with.

The unlimited resource within me was and is my Friend and my Teacher to which I do surrender even though I am merged with it. I found that my happiness was in giving everything I had away and learning to love. I no longer sought validation or anything but this Unnamable One and gave away everything that I had come to understand.

My surrender and enlightenment was based on a kind of spiritual reprieve brought to me depending on my daily spiritual condition. This condition was always kept high by keeping as priority the searching and the finding of that Source and giving away what I had to give.

These things I share with you like many things I shall share with you. In my experiences you will find many things similar to yours, although not everything. In the sharing of these things, your heart will grasp the light in it and the shadow self will magnify by that light that you might recognize its hidden presence looming in the dark. Having faced the real true issues of the shadow self as the source of the problem and by facing the light as the solution, then you may be granted your ascension on the basis of your daily spiritual condition.

In each day you may be granted reprieve from that aspect of the self which is the shadow self which masquerades as real. But it is really the aspect of one's being that has been created by living in a wounded world, believing in sickened principles.

You need to balance between that glorious kingdom and living here in this world. You must balance between the two dimensions otherwise one becomes too distant, not identifying with the people of this world. Acceptance of this brings ascension. The recognition through seeking and finding and ultimately letting go with total abandon to that resource which is no longer untapped. It is tapped at that point when there is total surrender to it.

All who seek it shall find absolute surrender in it, gradually or quickly, but all will find it. Each finds it in their own way, depending on their ability to be willing, open and honest. The willingness to acknowledge the shadow self and surrender it grows by asking who you are to become the servant to that indescribable power, which is extremely tolerant.

This unnamable and untapped resource is thought by so many to be very demanding, and in some ways that can be said to be true. But it is truly not demanding. It is truly permissive. It allows so much that human beings and others can set forward in this world. It is so permissive that it will allow many to go the wrong way, as I did.

Those who seek to surrender to this resource and ask for change may become more and more filled with it. Since it is infinite and goes on forever, then in each and every day, with each new circumstance and life experience, one may be granted this reprieve and embrace until such time as one is in total surrender and in their ascendant nature. The qualities of this are a joy and a total freedom.

There are those who are in this world in whom you shall see this. It is the unmistakable mark of God. They shall not be perfect; some of them will have tempers, or various quirks. They will be great or unnoticed people, but they shall have the marks of God: joy and freedom. They will express a beauty and a lightness and they will not be bound.

When you see them, recognize them as your brothers and sisters. Let them be your friends. In some instances, when they are teachers, humble yourself before them and ask them to show you the way and listen to what they say. They will be your companions. They will be sent to you by that unnamable resource that many term the Creator, God, the Supreme, or the Light. This will be your friend and you will see its word and sign in everything around you. Never waste your time in thinking or saying, 'I have heard this thing' or 'I know this thing,' Instead say, 'Thank you for reminding me. My Great One has chosen to reveal to me that this is what I need to hear again.'

This will be a part of your ability to stay receptive and it will be the chief way that you will remember to give away what you have. You will not be alone and you will be free. You are well on your way and the door is open. You have tapped that unnamable resource and you seek surrender to it. Yet the nature of surrender is only completely understood in that time when one has surrendered.

You have experienced joy and do experience it. There are days when it is easier to access and days when it is inaccessible. On those days, if you would still seek it and can come out of yourself and say, 'What can I do for another,' or 'what can I do for myself?' you will be guided where there is prayer and meditation. On those days you are in surrender, enjoy it and even announce it to the world. Say, 'Come with me, I know God. This day there is much to share of me. Here, those of you able to receive, I give this freely. Take this, for I keep my spiritual condition by giving it away.'

On those days you will know God and the voice of God's spirit shall be strong in you and teach you things and embrace you. The very next day it may not be there and you may be but an ordinary being. But where there is surrender, you will say, 'Thank you for this ordinary day.' There will be great appreciation and great fulfillment and no less joy. That will be the humility.

You will see many kinds of days. You will see many dimensions of your nature: greatness, smallness, perfection and flawed self. You will accept all of these. Your daily prayer will be, 'My Creator, take all of me, good or bad. Take all aspects of myself that stand in the way of my usefulness to you and my fellow humans. Grant me the strength as I go forward from here to do your bidding.' You will see that this great unnamable resource is your friend, for it is permissive. All things are allowed.

Karmas, however, may create action and reaction. But that is not the spirit of God. This is simply the Law. The Creator does not judge. The Law you would be wise to understand in that action begets reaction. Be ready to face all that needs to be cleansed and cleared by being ready and willing to face what needs to be faced.

Some days there are going to be great rewards, and other days there are amends to be made. These things are opportunities to finally clear with the Law until all things are cleared while you are still alive. Then the action/reaction response that some call karma no longer hurts or pains. You are free in yet another way for you have done the work.

You have come far, Anamika. What you have done is cleared much of the action/reaction response. This brings good things, but from time to time you may be surprised to find some opportunities to clear the decks as it were. These things shall be there, but we who are Spirit shall be there too, for we love you and shall never abandon you. You shall recognize us as the angels who are sent to you. We shall attend to you, guide you and work with you. We shall always be there for you to call upon. We are your friends in spirit. Pray to that which exists beyond yourself.

Pray that you are able to make the necessary shifts into your greater and truer self. This shall be granted every day. You are the light and you have the light. Be with the light and remember that it is something for now. If it should pass, seek it again and it shall be for now again.

It shall grow easier and easier to find it and the seeking shall grow shorter and shorter. The light shall grow more and more satisfying and the reward shall be without end. The challenges will be great and small, but the rewards shall be the gifts which are unnamable in value. These priceless jewels which are freedom and joy shall be yours and you will know they are forever, never to be taken away. This is the journey you are on and you are currently in this very embrace.

"Thank you so much for sharing your story and for your encouragement, Yeshua. Last night in Sakkara I had a breakthrough and since then I have felt myself in that embrace of God. I stepped through the window and the loneliness and emptiness are not present at all today. I feel whole and filled with a radiant joy."

Yes, this is so, but keep stepping through that window. The window is not permanent, nor a plane that one steps through and then nothing further. It will keep presenting itself for you to step through. You are doing magnificently and will continue to do so. Simply continue the great willingness you have, the honesty with yourself and your great openness. We do not need to remind you to keep seeking, for that you will do. We do not need to remind you to give away what you have, for that is your life. We do not need to remind you that from time to time things do come up to clear, for that is all too obvious.

The thing we must remind you of, and the thing that is the greatest blessing I have ever received is the reminder to keep stepping through the windows as they appear. For as simple as that sounds it is perhaps the easiest thing to forget. That spiritual condition is like a daily reprieve that is based on your willingness to keep stepping through. It is easy, it will be marked by joy and you will see it.

Recognize where you see and hear the voice of God. It comes from everywhere, the likely and the unlikely places. When you see it, speak to it even aloud and say, 'I heard the voice of God in you.' This will inspire them. Your light and all that you have earned and embraced will then serve them as well. You are well on your road and the joy is very present in your voice. My blessings are with you, dearest one.

CHAPTER 17

The Gift of Compassion

Inside of you, all there will be is light.
That light will be your treasure,
your true and real gift. - Sun Bear

My joy persisted and I was continually flooded with divine love and bliss. In this state, I was drawn more and more to Christopher. I wanted our relationship to become intimate. I knew it would not be long-term because there were many levels on which we could not relate to each other, but we had a powerful connection. Christopher understood me spiritually in a way no one else around me could. He could recognize my deep connection to other realms. He could sense and honor my primary relationship with God.

My decision to become intimate with Christopher confounded my mother and created a breach in our relationship. "Have you gone completely crazy? You have a Ph.D. and the man is an idiot! He doesn't earn a speck of money! He dresses like a slob and he can't even put an intelligent sentence together! What could you possibly see in him?" She wasn't wrong that Christopher and I did seem ill suited to each other.

Even though her logical evaluation of the situation was accurate, there were other reasons that made our being together right for a time. To her great consternation, I stood my ground because I needed the healing balm of Christopher's tender sweetness. So for a period of time, I gave my heart to him.

In the midst of the beauty that was unfolding for me, an ex-client reappeared and sued me for malpractice. I had worked with her for almost a year and had terminated the relationship when I found myself losing my professional perspective and being drawn into her drama. It was now two years later, and she was suing me for several hundred thousand dollars. Vicious fears of being persecuted, punished, publicly humiliated and financially wiped out hit me in the face full force.

After much wrangling with her and with her lawyer, I hired a lawyer who was able to resolve the matter. Protracted negotiations resulted in her acceptance of our offer to return all the money she had paid me for therapy. I was happy to do this as it seemed a good way to make amends and sever all connection.

However, my ex-client also wanted me to sign a confidentiality agreement while refusing to sign one herself. This meant that I could never reveal her name to anyone but it did not prevent her from smearing my name in any way she chose to. My lawyer was emphatic that I should not do this and counseled me that I should only sign the agreement if she signed one as well.

His advice was well founded and reasonable, totally in keeping with legal precedence. However, beyond having the damage repaired, which did occur, she was caught in a closed loop of revenge. Her vengeful and unforgiving view of reality could only be assuaged if I granted this unbalanced settlement. I could sense that the very instability that had caused me to drop her as a client required that I make this concession to bring the matter to a close. Despite her intention to prove me wrong and seek revenge, I was tempted to ignore my lawyer's advice and not insist on a reciprocal agreement.

Uncertain as to what to do, I sought advice from the Guides. They advised that I meditate deeply on the subject and listen to my heart. Following their suggestion, I went into a deep meditation for insight on this thorny issue. I quickly received the inspiration and almost without volition wrote: "This is my love letter to you, God. I entrust my care and well-being to you. I stand nakedly before you. I have your love and that is all I need. I place one hand on my heart and my other hand on your heart. How is it that both hands end up in the same place?"

A voice spoke back: *Thank you for entrusting me with your life, Anamika. We are together now, you and I. You are my passion, my devotion, my everything. My joy knows no bounds. You never again need to be afraid, for what I am, you are and we are one.*

That was all I needed. I picked up the pen and signed the legal document without the confidentiality clause that would legally protect me. I felt the rightness of it in my heart. I wanted to give my ex-client my trust knowing that it was in the highest for both of us and hoping that it might help her heal. I knew that God was my protector over and above the law and I joyously and nervously thrust the document in the mailbox hoping to be done with it.

To my great relief, my instincts turned out to be correct. I never again heard from her, nor did I hear of her defaming me in any way. When I thought about it years later, I was happy that I had listened to my own heart in making the decision instead of doing what everyone else thought I should do. This reinforced my newfound trust in my connection with God.

With this frightening episode behind me, I eased into a time of peace. Christopher and I decided to live together as our relationship was soothing and healing to my ravaged heart. This was truly a happy time in a sweet innocent way. My days were simple and free. I followed my inner impulses in each moment to determine what to do next. Most of my time was unstructured and life seemed to just flow. We moved into a beautiful house on the ocean and gathered there several days a week with the community of friends and family which had gradually come together. It was a gentle time full of love.

Mataare and I were still not close, but I was able to let it be, realizing that our connection was eternal, even if at times strained. I was still able to consult with the Guides periodically and hoped that eventually our personal friendship would return.

However, after each phase of peace came another torrent of pain with its ensuing shedding of layer after layer. This time I knew I must give my heart to the world and let it break.

Inside of me, mountains of fear and resistance emerged. I was afraid of being on this Earth. I was afraid to allow my heart to truly open with nothing held in reserve and no secret place to retreat for protection. It would take great courage for me to open myself and allow my heart to break, but I felt I had no choice; I had come too far to stop now.

"Okay God, I will give my heart to the world." Just as I said these words, the thunder began to rumble outside. As the storm's winds raged, I let the elements help break my resistance apart. I felt my being split wide open as the thunder clapped and lightening streaked to the ground in jagged, cataclysmic bursts.

Through this new space I felt a well-worn cloak of personal history dropping off behind me. Thus unencumbered and cleansed, I opened my heart, "God, I give you everything."

As I said these words a grief welled up in my chest and I wept as I let go of all I had known as myself. The heavens cracked open with a deluge of rain that flowed in harmony with the torrents of tears that fell upon my chest. I felt laid bare, with nothing left but the knowledge of my essence. I am Woman, Goddess, Teacher, Lover, Sister, Daughter and Divine Mother. My heart is the heart of the world.

An unbearable compassion flowed through me that made my soul weep, yet filled me with joy. In this divine feminine love, I felt strangely, yet deliciously, unattached to the world. Paradoxically, in giving forth my heart, I had come to be even more in the world and yet even less of it.

Later in Sakkara, I remembered again that compassion was all that mattered. The highest love that I could ever wish to achieve in human form was absolute compassion for everyone and everything no matter what darkness presented. "Please help me become a being who is able to live from a heart of compassion and give it to the world," I asked beseechingly.

As I uttered this prayer, I felt compassion enter my heart with a tremendous rush. My heart was full to bursting. The Guides whispered that because I had awakened my desire for the compassion within my own heart, they were able to amplify it for me. This beautiful compassion was my birthday gift.

As my birthday rolled around, I realized that two years had passed since Mataare and I had each symbolically married God. So much had happened. I could not recognize myself as the same person who naively made those vows. I had come far and nothing could turn me back now. The Guides granted me a birthday reading. This time it was Sun Bear who came to speak with me.

You are at the point of no return. That is, when one has had enough spiritual experiences, from that point forward they cannot go backwards because they have realized so much. From this point or any point forward it could be complete for you.

There is nothing reasonable about love. Love is an unreasonable, unfathomable power. You are moving from the reasonable to the God consciousness. This requires an extraordinary amount of surrender.

You have a great, great work to do in this world. Soon the energy to do this work will seem to be coming from all around you. The power and grace within will no longer only be internal. They will be mirrored everywhere within and without. This is where the calm will come from, and that's the maturity of your Avatar nature. What you now label an up or a down will be a joy. It is already happening.

Many people have expected a great tribulation on Earth at this time with many Earth changes. But, the two percent who have recognized the need for change have become so dynamic that they have caused a shift. Because of that, the Earth will not have to go through all of the shifts and destruction that were predicted, even though there will be much turbulence. But, so many people are looking forward to destruction that they created an archetype, which is beginning to form a separate reality where destruction is true. Many people on the Earth will die to be born in that other reality and get to live out their dream of destruction. The world will be going on a new path until more than two percent can get the message so that it can fulfill its higher destiny.

The higher consciousness of people actually holds the land masses up. That's why you and Mataare and others are in Florida, to hold it up. You can look toward moving on to a new place where you are needed. You must go and establish light in other places.

You have been given a very powerful and clear gift, Sakkara. You're supposed to do something with it. Sometimes you will have no idea what you are doing with it. It slowly will become clear why you have been given this specific gift and what it is for. Then, you can create a wonderful light in this world, which will have its own momentum.

Through learning to use your gift, you go through issue after issue until you are filled with grace. Inside of you, it gets smoother and smoother, even though the outside world may be filled with challenges. Then, you experience feeling united consistently with the Great Spirit and you will have a very powerful message for the world because you have been there and will share your experiences.

Inside of you, all there will be is light. That light will be your treasure, your true and real gift. The reason the Great Spirit gave you this particular power called Sakkara was so that it could be used to find your true light. By you giving away this gift, you get a potent revelation, which is to find the true and real gift inside of you.

After my reading, I basked for a while in the glow of the Guides, remembering the many things they had said to me. Had they hinted that I would be moving soon? I had the distinct feeling that that was exactly what they had done. At that moment I felt so at peace that moving again did not seem to be a particular challenge. If I was time to go, I would.

The doorbell rang, interrupting my musings. To my surprise it was a messenger with a dozen white roses and two birthday cards. I placed the roses on the table and sat down in front of them to open the cards. One of them was from Mataare and the other was from Sun Bear. Apparently Sun Bear had jumped into Mataare's body in the middle of the night, driven Mataare's car to a 24-hour store and had selected a card to honor my birthday. I was deeply moved by their caring.

"The Earth vibration"

CHAPTER 18

The Double Yammy Theory

Make the decision to be willing to continue to be
shown that which can be accessed
by the super conscious wisdom, which is
your being. – Philos

Mataare came to stay for a week. He had softened some of the outer layers of his wall but kept the central girding in place. Despite the remaining distince between us, we had an urge to talk to eachother. We were both feeling a great sense of anticipation, as though a new phase of our lives was about to unfold.

As we engaged in the long discussions that had become a central feature of our relationship, we discovered that both of us had been receiving messages that it was time to move. I told Mataare that the name Santa Barbara, California kept popping up and described to him some of the messages I had been receiving.

One day a drunken, disheveled man appeared out of nowhere on the beach in front of my house. He kept beckoning for me to come out and speak with him. He said he had spent the last twenty years traveling up and down the coast of California. I asked him where he thought I should move. "Montecito," he said. "It's a section of Santa Barbara." As I was mulling this over, he instantly disappeared. One moment he was there, and the next he was gone as mysteriously as he had appeared.

That night I also received a phone call from Gabriella who said she had recently moved to California. She was living in someone's six million dollar mansion and insisted that I absolutely must come and visit. When I asked where in California it was that she was living, she replied, "Montecito, it's a section of Santa Barbara."

The next morning, as I was dressing, a white blouse that I hadn't worn in a long while literally flew off the hanger into my hands. The label, which I had never noticed before, seemed to jump out at me. The name of the clothing company was Santa Barbara. "Ok, Ok I get it," I said aloud to no one in particular.

As Mataare and I talked, I realized that it seemed like I had been on hold for a year and a half. True, I was doing necessary healing work, but I was now ready to begin my real life's work. Inside, I was preparing to move on and I could see that the messages to move to Montecito reflected this inner movement. With Mataare there, I got the courage to speak to the Guides about my relationship with Christopher. I could sense that it would soon be over.

I had been feeling ambivalent about Christopher for a while. There were times that I just could not stand to be with him another minute as the differences between us that had so extremely exasperated my mother now mattered to me much more than they had in the beginning.

At the same time, I felt incapable of letting him go. I had fears of loss and terrible jealousy arising. Even though I was thinking of letting the relationship go, I was possessive of Christopher and I didn't want to see him with anyone else. This made no logical sense, yet it was the way I felt.

You must acknowledge that the reason you are in this kind of beautiful yet incomplete relationship is that something inside of you is not prepared to receive the thing that you say that you want. It has to do with coming down to Earth in personal love. You have made your picture of a soul mate a God and that doesn't exist in the form of a person.

In other words, you want him to be everything that you want for yourself but you are not sure you are that. Where you are not sure of your own identity, it keeps you from connecting with someone who does not match your picture because by association you feel that if you are with that kind of person it reflects on you. It feels like you are who you are with. This is standing in the way.

That is part of why you are with Christopher, who is so different than you. It is to get past the image, feel the love that is there and know that you are two different people. Those differences neither hold you back nor get you to go forward so long as you are not trying to make him different than he is. Everyone is advanced in an accepting connection like that.

So, you need to find the full manifestation of your own self-expression and become confident and happy with yourself. Then your soul mate can appear. Another approach is to accept that where you are in your current relationship is really the best you are able to create at this time. Your acceptance that where you are is really who you are right now will allow your soul mate to appear. Or, your self-acceptance can create the deep satisfaction that you are wanting in a relationship with the person you are with right now. This occurs from happiness with yourself.

My first reaction to these words was a great yearning to feel happy in myself and in relationship. Right on the heels of this yearning was a sense of loss. I realized that I was sad because what I had with Christopher was no longer working. This caused me great sorrow because I was once again losing a beautiful relationship that no longer served the highest. It was similar to what I had experienced with Isaac; two beautiful men in ultimately limited relationships. I knew I had to let go.

"What I want, whether it is with Christopher or not, is to experience the depth of that unconditional love within me and also in relationship."

Will you let the Creator do it in Its own way? If you will, you'll have that. But that may involve many factors you didn't plan. You must ask the Spirit of the universe not to let your cravings control what is right for you. Creator will put those in balance for you and you'll be able to cope with what goes on. Then, the right thing will result. Your life will be put into order for you. It takes a trust and a willingness to allow Spirit to manifest through you in a very flexible paradigm.

"I'm so afraid to let go because I don't trust that I'll be brought to something higher. My linear mind knows that every time I have let go, the next relationship, the next house, the next form of Sakkara always gets better, but it still terrifies me to let go. I just don't trust that there will be more love. I fear that I'll lose something."

"When the time comes for a change, what if I make the wrong decision? I feel if I make the wrong choice I might never find love and never find God on a deeper level than where I am now, which is not ultimately satisfying. Christopher will go off and be with someone else he loves and somehow I will never find the love that I want. That's my deepest fear, it's much worse than dying. I'm not afraid of dying, I'm afraid of living without love. Is holding onto this relationship blocking my true soul mate from coming?"

If Christopher were gone, there would still be a block in you. Until the block is gone, it will always be something. The block in you has nothing to do with you and Christopher whatsoever. The block is not yet being ready to have an unconditionally loving relationship, but a desire for a relationship that meets certain conditions. Therefore, the eye for that and the power to create that is aimed in the wrong direction.

Forget about a soul mate and love the one you're with without limit or control. If you can't do that then you must accept that this is where you are.

Ananika – Read it to

Love the one you with without limits an/or control.

That is why things are in this state of affairs. In the meantime, love each other. If you are unable to love each other because it gets so far outside of your conditions, then that's the time to part.

I heaved a sigh of relief. Their advice made such sense. While anticipating that a parting was coming, I settled into the mutual warmth that was present now.

Very soon, however, our lack of harmony had reached the breaking point. It no longer felt right for Christopher and I to have a primary romantic and sexual relationship. However, we still loved each other and wanted to remain close, yet the fears of making this change seemed overwhelming as I set out to Santa Barbara for my first visit.

Gabriella welcomed me into the enormous six million dollar villa in which she was staying. Gabriella and I share the same birthday and could always read each other with impeccable clarity, like my mother and I could. She had been with me when I was deciding to part from Isaac and she had parted from her partner at the same time. I poured out my heart to her, my pain and my fears and she understood it all. I heard the clear voice of God speaking to me through her. Then, much to our mutual surprise, my situation with Christopher catalyzed in her the very same relationship situation I was facing. It was time for her to let go of her partner as well.

We spent hours together facing our respective situations, wondering how we could accomplish letting go while avoiding collapsing into fear. We wanted to transmute the pain of separation into unconditional love and to be so full within ourselves that we could love with less attachment to the particular form. That is, we would be able to continue to be close and loving with our soon to be ex-partners as non-primary soul mates, and be delighted and supportive of a new person in their lives. A tall order? Yes, but there was nowhere else to go.

Gabriella and I cloistered ourselves in the mansion and spent days laughing, crying and encouraging eachother. Little by little, with each passing day, there were moments of reprieve before the next wave hit. Revelation after revelation began to replace the pain. These revelations went beyond intellectual understanding of the ideas and touched the place of that divine spark within. They promised a freedom and love that went far beyond the limitations of conditional love.

I had always believed in unconditional love and had felt many moments of it, but the fear of loss, jealousy and possessiveness that permeated my life had prevented me from living in that experience for prolonged periods of time. Gradually, as Gabriella and I worked through the maze of our current limitations, I began to experience an acceptance of myself for where I was and for Christopher as he was. It even seemed possible to accept him with someone else.

Sun Bear and Merlin explained to me that I was going through a death and was rebirthing myself as a totally new being:

It isn't within your current identity to carry out what's required. Therefore, see where your current identity seems to fall short and ask the Great Spirit to address that. If you do this simple thing, what stands in the way will be removed. The gift of a new self shall then exist there.

This is done by simply allowing Creator to continue the psychic transformation rather than you deciding that you are unable to go on. Make the decision to be willing to continue to be shown by the super conscious wisdom, which is your being, that which can be accessed. You might feel that you are drawing upon your own strength, but rest assured that you are drawing upon the strength in the universe. Be willing to allow that to emerge and to reinforce the psychic change. You are being pushed through a tube into your ascendant nature.

Sun Bear and Merlin also suggested that I do a completion ceremony with Christopher in order to keep my intentions clear and free me to step once again through a doorway to open further to my ascendant nature. With all my pain around leaving him, this seemed a daunting task, but I was determined to find the strength to do it when I returned to Florida.

One thing had become clear to me; the pain I was feeling was in fact leading me somewhere. I also remembered that this was now the time of year when the window of opportunity for ascension was most open. For the past two years during this period I was carried into the light. Clearly, I had not yet been ready to stay in the light, and was inexplicably drawn back into the pain and fear. This, the third time, might be different. Perhaps now I would be able to go all the way and claim my ascendant self. I was determined to strengthen my courage and increase my faith.

With my vision now clearly set on ascension, I found a pool of resentment toward God surfacing. I ranted and raved at God, "Why have I have to face so much pain all of my life? Why can't I have what I want? Why is this so hard?" I felt like Yeshua saying, "Why have you forsaken me?"

Then, I turned my anger inward, "How could I be so stupid? How could I allow myself to go through so many years of the same kind of experience over and over and still not get it? Why am I forever subject to the same miserable, limiting emotional responses?" I felt too angry about all of the pain to forgive myself for being where I was. I began beating myself up and heaping on self-blame.

Finally, I asked for help. "Lift this self-hatred and teach me forgiveness and compassion toward myself. Since we all have to go through the stages, step-by-step, help me move beyond my expectation of perfection. Help me accept my human failings. Help me accept my dark side."

As I asked for this acceptance of my human condition I could feel a change begin to take place. I felt more at peace and detached from the fear while also feeling a greater love toward Christopher. In this love, I felt the possibility of truly supporting him on his life path, even if that took us apart. What I wanted most was for his soul to evolve so that he could be happy. That was more important than the form our relationship took.

While I had always intellectually understood this way of thinking, I began to experience this truth as more important than my pain and loss. I saw that it was all divinely orchestrated for our highest awakening, not as punishment because God cares who sleeps with whom. It only matters that we embrace more love.

"Creator, I ask for all fears of lack, jealousy, possessiveness, self-hatred and attachment to be removed or accepted so that I can fully awaken to unlimited and unconditional love. I recommit myself to going all the way; I will not stop now."

All too soon, it was time for me to go home and face what awaited me. Gabriella and I reluctantly parted at the quaint little Spanish tiled Santa Barbara airport. We blessed each other on our respective journeys. We knew that we would be seeing each other again soon as it was now evident that Montecito was to be my next home. While I had trepidation about the upcoming changes and the loneliness it seemed I would face, I felt a growing strength and peace within me.

On the airplane, I took a stretch and went into the bathroom. As I turned toward the mirror I saw a beautiful woman. I did a double take to see who was in the bathroom with me. Since no one else was in the close quarters of the airplane bathroom, I looked again and there it was again. I wasn't used to seeing my own beauty, and yet, there it was. I had changed and softened. Some of the hard edges were gone. I could see the love and compassion in my eyes, and I could feel God's love which was one as the same as my own love radiating forth from me.

I felt no lack for the moment, only abundance, as I realized that I was not losing anything. I was simply stripping myself of the fears that kept me feeling separated, kept me from experiencing the fullness of love. Without the harsh self-judgment looming that was usually there I realized that all of us, including me, are doing the best that we can. Tentatively, I allowed myself a few more morsels of self-acceptance, realizing that I did have tremendous courage and faith, a commitment to do whatever it takes and a capacity to experience real love.

These thoughts brought comfort because this new state of self-acceptance was so fragile. It needed to unfold in its own time with simple gratitude for whatever is now.

A smile crept over my face. I thought, "You know, I could end up wild, crazy in love," and best of all, it would be love for myself. "I totally put myself in your hands, God. I trust you more deeply now. As I let go of the control, please carry me home."

Christopher had moved out of the house while I was away. My first night at home sleeping alone passed uneventfully. However, by the next day some terror surfaced and I felt completely insignificant and irrelevant to God. It was as if I may as well not exist at all. I felt that my existance didn't matter and I wanted to die. Not that I wanted to kill myself, I just didn't want to exist.

This space was black and deep, but gradually an inner light dawned as I emerged from the terror. Not only was I not insignificant, but I am "the One" to my God just as everyone else is "the One". I saw that I had been searching for "the One" to fulfill me outside of myself because I had not before realized that I was one with "the One." I saw that there was no one more precious and special to God than I was, and that this was uniquely true for everyone. There is more than enough love since it is indeed infinite.

As the Guides had suggested, Christopher and I created a beautiful completion ceremony in the presence of our caring community. We pledged our eternal love to each other. We acknowledged the beauty and importance of the journey we had taken together. We honored each other, spoke our need to go in separate directions, released each other in love and exchanged beautiful purple-pink strawberry calcite stones symbolic of our bond. This was done through many tears, much love and deep gratitude.

Literally fifteen minutes after the ceremony ended, Christopher was in bed with another woman. Even though I had more than suspected it would happen this way, his actions were my worst nightmare come true. It was the one thing I thought I could not endure; yet I had to face this too. I knew that he had to do this. His psyche was too fragile to withstand the separation without holding on to another woman. The alternative to his actions would have been his total demise, which I would not have wanted to see happen.

Holding the perspective of this revelation did help immensely. Yet, the wounded possessive part of me still viewed him as my man. I couldn't help but feel that he was being unfaithful to me, even though we had terminated our sexual relationship. I screamed, cried, wanted to punish him and wanted to kill her. I asked God for help to let go and to show me unconditional love.

In my pain, I never wanted to see Christopher again but my heart would not allow that as I did truly love him.I realized that I didn't need to let go of him; I needed to let go of my attachment to him. Since I was determined to learn unconditional love in the face of my deepest wound, I wanted to find a way to love Christopher for exactly who he was, not who I wanted him to be.

After a time my hysteria subsided to the point that I was able to think more clearly. I knew that this pain was my opportunity to open and step through to a new place. I could feel God's presence comingled with me so strongly that all I needed to do was focus inwardly and ask for a higher revelation each time the pain came.

I noticed that as long as I stayed in divine love, all else was handled with ease and the pain ceased, it didn't exist in that place. If I left the love space, then fear of lack, loss and separation would engulf me and wrench my guts. The unconditional love felt joyous, open and liberating. When I could hold my focus gently there, I was home.

I claimed this inner home and my inner portal to the Infinite. I claimed my right to experience divine love and I proclaimed my desire to walk the planet as an instrument of that love. As I claimed this birthright, it was as if a faucet was turned on and I was standing under an open tap. I felt my cells dying and transmuting into a new life as they were stretched to make room for all of the new energy. Through this process, I realized how much more connection was possible with God. Here was a chance to open to divine love as never before.

Later, in Sakkara, I looked over at Christopher and felt the tears well up inside of me because of the loss of him as my lover. The tears were also the grief of having experienced the loss of my own God connection for millennia. Inwardly, I continued to claim my source, my love and my birthright.

Then, I looked at Christopher again and felt a deep love along with a strange detachment. I could truly see him for who he was without projecting an image onto him of who I needed him to be. I knew that I would love this man forever, but that we were not the right match for a primary relationship and I felt a peace in letting go. I sent a silent prayer that we each be led to the highest path for our growth.

With that prayer, a gentle, sweet and peaceful compassion infused the room. The Sakkara ended tenderly. Several of us stayed afterward to chat when something very strange occurred. In mid-sentence, I found myself carried into a space in which my personality self disappeared. Aside from a fleeting concern that I might have gone crazy, I was not afraid even though my entire human self was nowhere in sight. It was as if I were pure God essence, experiencing reality from a new vantage point. I had no human emotions, no concerns, no thoughts, nothing. I just was. I could vaguely remember having had a personal history, but I had no connection with it and no feelings about it. It seemed entirely irrelevant. For the moment, the personality self Anamika no longer existed. I was in the world, but utterly detached from it.

As I was noting all of this, someone looked at me and called my name. I heard myself reply, "That's not my name."

"What is your name, if not Anamika?" she inquired, quite frankly puzzled.

"My name is God-Self," I replied. I sat awake in this state most of the night simply being. When morning broke I was gently reintegrated with my human personality self. Surprisingly, I was relieved to receive Anamika back. "I kind of like her," I thought, "despite all of her quirks and problems."

More importantly, I felt gratitude for this human self. I liked being human after all! I realized that I could not exist or maneuver in the world without a persona. The God-Self needed a vehicle in which to get around and I was so glad I had one!

While I felt more appreciation of being human, simultaneously there was a greater detachment from the drama, from the ups and downs of the human condition. Gradually, over the next several days as I became more comfortably reintegrated in my human self, new lessons began to appear.

One morning I awoke angry. When I delved into it, I discovered that I had been judging myself and making myself wrong for my feelings, emotions and for just being me. "Who says it's better to feel joy than sorrow? Who says it's wrong to feel fear?" I asked myself. For a moment in time I suspended all judgment and thanked all of my darkness as well as my light. I dared to accept all of me. The crippling self-rejection and self-judgment were momentarily suspended.

Suddenly, I experienced an inexpressible joy and freedom. This is it, this is it! The Buddha's presence was with me and I understood from deep inside his particular enlightenment, his revelation. In a flash he had understood that he was completely fine the way he was, all of him. There was no need to be any other person, or any different than who he was or where he was.

I began to repeat, "I am who I am. I am where I am." It felt like the singsong of a little child, "I yam who I yam. I yam where I yam." This little child was singing the truth about her life, her Yam Theory as she called it, "I yam who I yam." Her Yam Theory then expanded into the Double Yammy Theory to include both who and where I yam. I laughed, promising her that I would remember that her Double Yammy Theory was the key to a joyous existence.

CHAPTER 19

ANOINTED

Spiritual ascension requires a surrender to that Supreme Intelligence and a letting go completely to the guidance of that inner light which is free of all personal ambition, drive and directive. – Yeshua

Ascension Day arrived once again. I called Mataare for my traditional Ascension Day reading. As was customary on this day, Yeshua was the one who came to address me.

Spiritual ascension requires surrender to the Supreme Intelligence. It requires letting go completely to the guidance of that inner light which is free of all personal ambition, drive and directive. That is why so few have shifted into that consciousness, for rare is the soul who wants to give up their own personality to discover what is revealed by the Source.

In order to complete one's human life, one must be prepared to complete the karmas of all of their existences. In order to do this, one must discover an altruistic love which will move into an unconditional love. When a soul is so full of love that they can give to others before themselves, they amass enough power to pay their karmic debts. This allows them to complete their human life.

They must be prepared to go to any lengths to fill themselves with such love when needed, so that they are able to give unselfishly. This takes them beyond that very natural state of self-centeredness that every human being experiences. The natural human self, while still in a human body, must surrender to an unnatural human state of ascendant awareness. When a sufficient number of beings make that shift, it becomes possible for many, many more to enter that doorway.

This ascendant state cannot be aspired to, for aspiration stands in the way. However, one can devotionally approach the Supreme through the inner doorway of their being and ask the Supreme to remove from them their own self-centeredness. Ask to be made an instrument of the Divine. Ask to bring peace and light into this world, with no thought of the self, but for that which includes all.

In no way does this kind of consciousness match or parallel what is motivating to the natural human being. It is only motivating to those who have touched such supreme awareness that that creates within them a desire for that kind of love. They are driven to the ascendant self with a desire for that supreme love as a result of their divine experience. Plus, in the outer world, they have found that every other kind of love has failed them.

It is important for the soul to make a decision to surrender their being to the Cosmic Truth as they have come to understand it, no matter how limited. As a result of making that decision, the necessary acts of surrender will come. That soul then has to stop fighting and struggling with the world and everyone in it for that only creates more to account for later, more to set right, more to complete. If one cannot stop fighting, one asks the Supreme: "Show me the way. I'd rather be about the business of completing."

After this is done, one can then see that everything that happens to them each day is an opportunity to settle affairs. Then one by one by one, each and every affair is settled ultimately with the most unconditional love that one can find. For each soul this is a different amount.

This is the path that you are upon. Every experience you have, whether you can or can't remember the matter generating in this or another life, is so that you can settle affairs. It exists for you to go into your divine nature and ask, "How might I love unconditionally? How might I give what needs to be given? How might I clear and complete? How might I give the powerful light that I have come into this world with? How might I minimize all that interferes with me giving this contribution so that I can be effective to more?"

I come to be with you so that you might carry this light, and to make things just right according to your vision. We are here for the express purpose of helping you find that road that moves you forward and deeper into the light so that you can enjoy your existence here and complete it.

Do not develop strong desires for that which exists in this world. Do not cultivate existing desires but simply ask the Spirit to address them. Desires are not wrong or bad to have. In fact, many of them are quite good. But if you cultivate the existing strong desires, then you will be taken away from the truest focus. Then, all of your great power will be focused in ways which will set things all atumble. That power flowing in directions other than altruistic will then cause a great crashing in your personal life. But, if directed by the vast Spirit of which you are a part, that power will cause a great lifting, or ascension. This is the meaning of ascension. These strong desires must be left entirely to the vast Spirit of the universe to address since you have made a decision to surrender.

"Yeshua, are you telling me these things because there is something off track or to remind me to stay on track?"

Ananika
Issues

I am telling you for both reasons. There are two things off track. One is ambition, or the need for validation from your true peers, and the other is the focus on soul mate. That which is on track is your devotional surrender, your enlightenment, the passing on of unconditional love to those who are able to receive it, working with others to bring awakening for those who are able to receive it, and working with others to bring healing and shifting to those who are not yet able to awaken so that in the future they might be able to.

The two things off track are already shifting. Certain ambition can be altruistic but also quite contrary to the completion of true purpose. For example, my desire to reach every single soul in this world appeared to come from compassion. It was, in fact a reflection that I did not trust that there was a plan greater than I could see. This left me to think that I was the power and that I was the Source. It was, in fact, a powerful expression of ego and not unconditional love. In your case, the need to be recognized by the world and acknowledged by your peers, who are those who can affect the world in a powerful way, will stand in the way and is your greatest enemy.

As you go forward every single day you will be shown how those things still remain as a part of your being and you will need to ask for guidance. While you are in a physical body you are vulnerable to physical natures, which are not enemies. They are empowering dimensions of your being which are not good or bad, it just depends on how they are used.

Lack of freedom comes from either forcing yourself to do something that your psyche is not ready for, or fearing that you may never change. If you know that you will do what you can and the rest shall be what it will be, that is the freedom. Clearing or completing all residual energy doesn't mean handling every detail. It means being willing to handle what you can and letting go of what you can't.

You may never know the difference between who you are at the most magnificent level and a currently created ego. Sometimes they may be interchangeable. Yet it is the seeking of that expansion that causes it to happen. No human being is through the door all the time. The beauty comes from the fact that the quality of one's existence continually becomes simpler and better. That is how one becomes content and serene. Seeking less and finding more is how it works. But there are not always ways for you to accurately judge yourself against that standard for there are things in your life which are paradoxical and will remain unclear.

When you are done with most of your outer work in the world, it will be easier to assess yourself. But so long as you are still in a world that carries so much sickness and darkness, as a Master dedicated to the truth you will find yourself, without realizing it, taking on the image of the very darkness itself. In this way aspects which are in the darkness may identify with you and be carried out into the light. You won't always know whether it is your own darkness or the intent of the Creator that causes you to mirror the darkness. If your intention is the light it won't really matter.

The reason I am telling you all of this is that you have been anointed, Christed, to go through the doorway and you will need to know these things at various junctures now and later. You are in the doorway, and you have surrendered into a power which is taking you through even when you are not aware of it. You carry so much light that God will mend all of your errors simply because of your intention to help. Remember these words.

Anointed? Me? While I was experiencing miraculous changes, this seemed too good to be true. After listening to the reading with Yeshua, I put my whole self in Creator's hands yet again. "I give myself entirely to you, God."

Then, something happened. I was lifted into a freedom so light and joyous that I smiled and laughed. God's love poured through me. Suddenly I could see that it didn't matter how I felt or didn't feel. What mattered was to honestly admit it, accept it and turn it over. I felt the bliss of that liberation. Nothing mattered; it was all love. With this love as a reference point I was now ready to embark on the next phase of my journey, whatever it would bring.

CHAPTER 20

My Beloved

You are going right into the heart of God
over and over until what is manifested from you
thoroughly is pure God light. – Francesco

Just as synchronicities had quickly moved me from Boston to Sarasota nearly two years before, the same magical force moved me to California. When I first arrived in Montecito, I was mesmerized by its beauty. My house was a mountain retreat with an expansive view of the ocean. Shamuki and I hiked the steep windy trails spending hours outdoors, just breathing in the wonder of it all. Yet, I was so alone.

When I had moved to Florida some of my family had lived there and before long I also had friends, a lover and a committed group of Sakkara participants. I had relatively quickly built a community and eventually was busy and fulfilled just as in Boston. It never occurred to me that I was supposed to do it differently in Florida than I did in Boston. I thought I had been idle long enough and so began to recreate my life.

Here in California I was beginning at square one and knew no one but Gabriella. I had felt that because I had let go of Christopher and was coming to California to start a new life that my true soul mate would appear. The Guides had hinted that he would be coming soon and I was looking for him everywhere. The old familiar terror began rising in me again and I had the grave realization that I was not as clear as I had thought. "Oh, God, not again," I moaned as the emotional well sprang open and the constant crying began again. I called on the Guides and Francesco came to speak to me.

You are indeed facing much to cry about, for you are not doing what is ordinary. You are being asked to shift to yet another dimension. Your obstacle is not that you refuse to shift. It is the pain that arises from the fear of loss when you have nothing else to replace what you had. It is the belief that there is not enough for you. This prevents you from letting go. Ask Spirit to show you that there is enough. Ask for help to rid yourself of the obstacle that is preventing you from experiencing the next dimension.

You are being recreated as a human being in the image of the Divine so that you may enter our dimension. In this reality you will be able to live happy, joyous, and free. Not being happy, joyous, and free leaves you in bondage. Say, 'Spirit of the universe, free me from my bondage to this old form which enslaves me.' Then you will experience being in the higher dimension while living as a human being.

Every Avatar fears that if they let go of their final bonds that it will somehow represent loss rather than gain. That is the final degree of their focus on themselves and their needs. This focus is the bondage that keeps one attracted to the Earth plane.

You need only a simple recognition that there is an obstacle to what you want. You must acknowledge that this obstacle is a pattern fueled by fear. The pattern causes you to clutch onto things because of a fear of loss. You are bound to that and need to ask for freedom from it so that you are free to move on to whatever is there.

You are doing a very wonderful thing and you are making a good and high choice. It just feels hard, but you are working it out. You did not realize how strong a hold this fear had on you. Soon you will have humor about its hold and that will be the beginning of your freedom. It may not make feelings of fear or jealousy go away, but you will be able to take that part of you less seriously.

We understand that this time is difficult, but you are involved in the business of completing, not recycling. The most beautiful thing is if you are able to forget yourself in the service to God. It was for this reason you were provided your healing gifts. Because of them, every matter in your life will be saved.

You are finding cosmic consciousness through the gifts you were given, through the need to be in the state of ecstasy, and through helping people experience that state. You are going right into the heart of God over and over until you thoroughly manifest pure God Light. That has already happened in so many ways in your life and will continue to happen more and more.

Francesco's words were comforting and uplifting. I began to see that my pain was taking me deeper into Source. Consequently, I was able to let go a little more and to ask for the Presence to be with me. I felt the Guides' help each day as I surrendered more and more of whom I had thought myself to be. Each day I examined my motives and identified the fear-based ones, asked for help with those and prayed to be of service. The emptiness gradually gave way to a gentle sweetness, peace, and joy. I was delighted and felt that I had finally arrived at the real beginning.

Confidently I requested, "Take anything and everything standing in the way of unconditional love." And, I was hit! A pain seared through my heart so deeply that I became engulfed with what felt like not only all of the pain of the world but all of the pain of existence itself.

There was nothing I could do to lift it. I screamed at God all day and night, "How can you allow this pain? How could you have done this to me if you say you love me? How do you expect us to live in this hell hole called Earth? Don't you care how we feel? I need your caring and compassion now!"

Gradually, I moved from being the victim of the pain to the owner of all the pain in the world. "All of this darkness is part of me." I finally conceded. "I contain revenge, deceit, dishonesty, depravity, jealousy, lack of integrity, betrayal, seduction, thievery, possessiveness, lust, desire, greed, fear of lack, insanity, hatred, manipulation, arrogance, superiority, inferiority, insecurity, demands, control, distrust, pride, guilt... I have it all in my soul, everything but murder in this life. Oh, what am I saying, I just killed a flea this morning. Yes, murder too. So what if I haven't killed a human in this life, I have had vengeful feelings of wanting to kill like wanting to kill Christopher's new girlfriend. Yes, I have it all! There's no darkness I do not have. I have been denying this all of my life, trying to be a "good" person. I claim this darkness in my soul. And if you can love me even now with all of this darkness, you are bigger than I am!" I completely disarmed myself by chuckling aloud as this last phrase came out of my mouth. Of course God is bigger than I am!

As I accepted the darkness, I found a freedom in admitting it all. Surprisingly, it ceased to feel badly. Yet, it didn't feel good either. In fact, I felt nothing. I was suspended in the center between light and dark. There was no pain and no joy. I had surrendered my old self for reshaping. The parts that had been taken had not yet been replaced with anything. In this suspended state, nothing mattered, not my lifelong quest for God consciousness, not even the search for my soul mate. None of it mattered, not in the slightest.

I was present in my human self, yet detached. I felt like a clear pane of glass, here simply to mirror what others needed to see. My personal needs, desires and attachments were not present as I sat suspended as no thing in nothingness.

In this state, I was utterly committed to and surprisingly able to be of service only. I did not think at all of myself and it was my greatest joy to give. I could now feel that the more love I gave, the more love I had. My self-centered concerns did not exist here.

On an impulse I opened the front door. There was a beautiful large yellow and black butterfly on the straw mat which seemed to be dying. The butterfly's spirit entered the room and was transformed into a large angel. It told me that it had come to inform me that I had indeed gone through a transformation.

As the spirit left the body of the butterfly and it physically died, I picked it up and gently carried it into the house with gratitude. I had received the message that this part of the journey was complete and a critical corner had been turned. I knew it was not the end of my journey. There was more to come, yet something had irrevocably changed.

For a while I allowed myself to be more small and helpless than I had ever been. I came to admit that there was truly nothing that I as a person could do without Source; I needed God for everything. I was utterly dependent. My finite self was too limited to ever attain either happiness or fulfillment. It was actually a relief to keep admitting the helplessness as well as the darkness.

Then, I had a reading with the Guides in which they unexpectedly teased me that my soul mate was coming and that it would be soon. This reading sent me reeling. After the initial shock and excitement wore off, I was plagued with doubts. I began to feel that their trickery must even include their prediction of the arrival of this long-awaited person. I became deathly afraid that it would never happen. Even if he did arrive he would never want me. I wasn't good enough, smart enough, or attractive enough. Every insecurity about myself surfaced, even long forgotten childhood ones as I plunged into a torrent of self-effacement.

I dared to dive below these insecurities and I came to feel that not only the life I had lived, but my entire existence itself was of no consequence. I was utterly, completely existentially invalid. I was consigned to a state of perpetual inconsequentiality. It wasn't that I wanted to die, because that wouldn't have helped. I wanted to cease to exist, as if I had never been.

I thought I had hit bottom before, but I now realized that there is never a final bottom. Falling into the abyss of pain and darkness would happen again and again and again. Why did I always forget this? Why did I always think that I was out of the pit, and would never have to face it again? I was never prepared when another layer arose. Life is not for the faint-hearted, I surmised. From the heights of the potential fulfillment of my dearest dream I once again dove into self-invalidating pain that was like the sting of a thousand scorpions.

My desolation was complete. I screamed to the mountains, "Take this pain, take my attachment to this idealized man, take my attachment to an idealized self. Help me to be me and to love myself for it."

In answer to my entreaties, unexpected joy captured me for no external reason whatsoever. It was love without a reason, unreasonable love. Miraculously, I experienced life itself as a romance with God as Constance had predicted years ago. That quickly, that easily, the pain that could have gone on for days, was gone.

My joy continued to unfold day by day. Life was not without its ups and downs and daily challenges, but as soon as I felt the challenge a solution would present itself in the form of some small miracle. I continued to be ruthlessly honest in scrutinizing my motivations to see which were fear based or self-centered. It became easier and easier to acknowledge these motivations as well as my mistakes, without any judgment. I began to feel truly loved and supported by God as I experienced love's presence in every action, each moment of the day.

In the midst of this miraculous joy, I experienced my own inner radiance to such a degree that I fell in love with myself all over again. While I had seen many glimpses of this over the years, I was now thrust into a full blown experience. I dared to view myself from outside, and saw perhaps for the first time what others saw.

In the face of this startling objectivity, it became painfully sobering that I had been fighting a lifelong battle through thick walls of self-hatred and self-perceived ugliness. I had never been able to understand why anyone would love me, find me beautiful or desirable. I couldn't imagine how my soon to arrive soul mate would be able to love me. It wasn't until now that the truth of who I am was sufficiently revealed to me that I could experience any real self-love. In this moment, I loved myself the way I imagined I would feel toward the most exquisite lover. I loved myself the way I loved God.

This revelation simplified life. I only needed to be myself and allow the radiance that I am to exude. It wasn't a matter of giving or serving or doing or fixing. This radiant beingness emanating forth was all that mattered.

I could not find a word for this concept; nothing quite described it. I thought of being of service, being a vehicle, an instrument or an agent of the light. I thought of being teacher of God, an emissary of the light, transmitting the light, or emanating one's presence. Nothing quite captured its essence, it was a concept beyond words.

Gradually and gently my heart began to open more and more. I was in love, in bliss, and in a state of grace with no effort. Laughter and joy were present throughout the day. Paradoxically, there was both purpose and purposelessness to all I did. I had never felt so soft, so surrendered, so nakedly open and yet so full all at once.

"God, whatever you would have of me is what I want. My heart is with you and my life is filled with your grace. Show me your heart's desire and it is mine."

The brilliance of what seemed to be a billion suns illuminated me and I felt the Divine Mother come into me. She cradled the whole planet in her gentle hands. She wept tears of sorrow that the people of the world could not weep for themselves. With a heart of compassion she enveloped her children in love.

The world is in such pain, let me help to ease it. Let my love flow through you like a river to give to the world. Their pain is my pain and they are hurting badly. Let me love them, touch them, and help them know joy. Hold your hands as a cup and receive God's bounty.

I cupped my hands and felt energy filling the container. I was wondering what I should do with this energy when I found myself spontaneously pouring it from the cup out to the people of the world. Tears of gratitude streamed down my face for the great compassion I felt from the selflessly giving heart of the Mother.

With all of the blissful frequencies coursing through me daily, I was still awaiting the arrival of my soul mate that the Guides had predicted. I spoke to about this and asked if there was something in me blocking his arrival.

There will always be some obstacle that arises. This is true, even if at some point it seems there is nothing. The obstacles that arise need to be a part of how one lives. They must not be seen as that which ends or prevents a relationship. They must be accepted as part of relating. They must not prevent a flow of love. By honestly speaking of one's doubts and by accepting the obstacles as they arise, you will attain deeper and deeper love.

What seems to have happened is your soul mate energy has arrived rather than the soul mate in the physical form. If he came into your life at this moment, some obstacle would arise that would make you feel that he was not the one. Consequently, we see the need to create a flow of love in supportive relationships of a less intimate nature.

At this moment there is a masked dagger that threatens you. It is quite naturally causing you to feel that there is something against which you must protect yourself. Your new person will arrive amidst the ones you already love. There has been an unaware deception between those who love each other and this must be cleared. They must be unafraid to love you deeper by admitting what lurks between you and them and you must receive it without rejection, but with gratitude.

You have been needing your soul mate to be someone who doesn't hurt you. You need for him to be someone who loves you just right. His love for you must be a perfect one. You know intellectually he can't be perfect, yet you act as if this perfection is a prerequisite quality. What if he doesn't deal with issues the way you want him to and he's still your soul mate? You still need to open to love in a way you haven't even considered because that place of acceptance inside of you has been so wounded that the imperfect love that your soul mate can offer you doesn't even seem like love to you.

It is necessary to keep on learning and being willing to have revealed to you what it is exactly that you need to do. You must be humble enough to not go into the cycle of thinking that you're not good enough, that you'll never get there and it will never arrive.

That is a defense that allows you to keep holding onto the ego attachment that recycles the syndrome that wants you and your soul mate to be perfect. This same ego attachment wants you to believe that you must be seen that way. This is tied into a sickness that must entirely be left behind because it blocks your happiness, your success and your soul mate. You are moving in that direction right now.

I began to ask the friends and ex-lovers whom I considered to be soul mates what prevented them from loving me more. The answers ranged from envy, to fear of rejection, to fear of being loved conditionally, to feeling like I couldn't receive their love. I absorbed the feedback and went directly to God with all of it. Day by day, even though my mood lightened and lifted, a terrible ache and tearing in my heart persisted.

There was one acquaintance for whom I inexplicably felt immense hatred. I had been dealing with this by ignoring her presence and shutting her out. This had done nothing to reduce my ill feelings towards her. As I sat quietly, I saw that she represented a part of me that I was rejecting, hating, and judging as unworthy of love. I decided to take her into my heart, despite my dislike.

I realized that anyone I had not been able to embrace with love was a piece of myself I had been judging as unlovable. I had never before taken each and every one of these unlovable pieces into my heart. I had rejected these parts as well as the people who represented them. I was, in effect, pushing away the mirror I could not tolerate. I had been holding the darkness at bay by rejecting the people, instead of taking these rejected parts of myself into my own heart.

As I drew the woman I had hated into my heart, a small ball of light formed there. I then brought all of my deepest soul mates and loves into my heart, and the ball of light began to grow. Soon it grew into a huge golden orb in my heart. The intensity of light within the orb began to grow until the pressure was so great that it exploded.

I remembered the Guides telling me that one day there would be an explosion in my heart. When it actually happened, this explosion created so much space where before there had been self-protection. Love came coursing through like a powerful river flowing in all directions at once.

Soon a drilling sensation began in my forehead which pierced through into the middle of my head and went up through the top. As it pierced the crown, a lotus blossom opened on top of my head, and I seemed to disappear into colorlessness. Rays of light shot out all around and a gentle peace washed over me.

"Welcome into me, God. I want you to feel safe and at home in my heart. I don't want you to feel judged, rejected or condemned. I know that pain. When you think of me I want you to know that you can rest there at home in my heart.

"I want my heart to be welcoming and beautiful so that you seek it out. I want my heart to be a safe haven for you, a shelter from the storm. I want my heart to be where you choose to be in your radiance. Please enter, the door is open wide and I welcome you in. I want you to feel loved. I've been gone too long from you and I ask your forgiveness. You are my devotion, you are my heart, you are the reason that I exist. You are everything to me. There is nothing that means more to me than you. I exist because of you, for you and through you. You are my Beloved."

CHAPTER 21

THE BRIDGE ACROSS DIMENSIONS

What you feel is beyond you is,
and the solution is in further surrender. – Merlin

My mother and I regained our close relationship and she was once again my best friend and confidant. It was difficult that she was living 3,000 miles away but we spent much time on the phone to make up for the distance. On October 25, 1995, my father's birthday, I received a shocking call from her. She told me that she had been diagnosed with inoperable pancreatic cancer and had been given only three months to live. Her call precipitated a series of events and actions on my part that changed my life forever.

My mother had been complaining of abdominal pains for months and I had known there was something amiss, but never thought it would be this. I immediately went into panic. If my mother died, my whole world would collapse.

When my mother and I finished talking, I hung up the phone in a numb, shocked state. After a while I came to my senses enough to remember to ask Spirit for help. I received a strong message that I needed to walk to a powerful place on the land in order to gain perspective.

Shamuki and I left the house and climbed a nearby mountain peak. I fell to my knees in the dirt sobbing to God, "I feel completely helpless. Please show me the way. I want my mother to live and if that is possible, please bring it about. If it is her time to go, help me to accept this and find peace. How can I use this crisis for her healing and the awakening of others as well?"

Through the fear and tears a vision began to form. It was a vision of an international call to healing, a worldwide network of light to help not only my mother but everyone. I thanked Spirit for this revelation and Shamuki and I went directly home to draft a message:

"A CALL TO HEALING: What would happen if on a specific day and time all people of the world joined in love, prayer, and meditation for individual and collective healing? When two or more are gathered in love, it opens the way for miracles to bless and shower our lives...."

The message spoke of who I was, my mother's illness and my vision of an awakening not only for her, but for all of humanity. I asked people to join in on Sunday, November 19th at noon EST for five minutes. During this time we would all ask for the help we needed and send our blessings.

I jumped into action and spent the next ten days in a faxing and phoning frenzy. Within a short time a network of light spread by word of mouth all over the world until my anticipated hundreds turned into an estimated fifty thousand. I was astounded by the powerfully loving response.

The day of the world healing arrived with a sense of expectancy. My family had gathered at my parents' home in Connecticut with fifteen minutes to go before high noon. We piled onto my mother's king size bed. She was propped up on overstuffed pillows leaning back on the headboard. My father and I cradled her like bookends, one on each side, while my two sisters and brother gathered close.

At five minutes before noon we began to prepare. One by one we spoke our intention for my mother's healing, our own healing and the healing of the world. At noon, a brilliant but gentle light began to fill the room. I sensed my mother's parents, both of whom were in spirit, drift in to hold her. I saw Yeshua take his place in the center of our family circle. The light began to intensify and I noticed the room filling with angels, Archangels and Guides. We were being infused with an exquisitely pure and radiant divine love which was palpable to all of us.

I glanced down at my left hand which was gently resting on my mother's abdomen above the pancreatic tumor. I saw what appeared to be the hand of God reaching through my hand into my mother's body to illuminate her darkness with a brilliant light. I watched as my mother drifted out of her body and had a vision. Gradually, while she was held in this reverie, a deep peace began to descend upon all of us as we awaited her response. After a while, my mother opened her eyes and said, "I feel I'm going to make it."

"What were you dreaming?" I asked her.

"Oh, funny you should ask. I dreamed that I went to the store to buy a pickle and I was wondering which way they would slice it."

We all looked at her puzzled. Here she was the focus of thousands of people all over the world and she was dreaming of pickles! A mischievous expression crossed her face, "Did you know that the pancreas is shaped like a pickle? I guess I was dreaming about slicing out the tumor." We all smiled. It was so typical of my mother's earthy, practical humor.

My attention was drawn back to the light and I felt the presence of God move through me to deliver beautiful, reassuring messages for each family member present. The messages were received amidst many tears. Then my family turned to me and asked, "What about you, Anamika? What is the message for you?"

I closed my eyes and the message came in the form of golden white cylinder of light that surrounded me like a spotlight. The unmistakable voice of God spoke, *You are the light of the world.* I burst into tears. I understood that God was saying that I was that light already and could therefore let go of any doubt that this was so.

The golden white light filled my heart with a quiet peace I'd never known. I felt touched by God from deep within. In answer to my prayers, the fear of my mother's death and the emptiness I assumed I would feel had somehow lifted for the moment. The hand of Grace was there comforting me whether she lived or died.

I gazed beyond the circle of my family. I saw seeds of light planted all over the world by the people participating in the Call to Healing. Inwardly, I gave thanks to those whose hearts were open and willing. Tears of profound gratitude spilled from my heart.

I glanced over at my mother. Her face had relaxed into a deep peace. She said, "For the first time, I can actually imagine making it through this illness." I knew this was true, but only if she wanted to.

Though my family put a lot of energy into my mother's healing, she was not taking charge of her own well-being This was a sharp contrast to her hopeful state of mind after the Call to Healing. With each passing day she was not getting better. It felt like we were dragging her along, trying to convince her to chose life. It began to become clear that she really didn't want to live.

As my recognition of this reality deepend, I became increasingly incapacitated by the fact that my mother might actually die. This realization made the lack of a partner in my life even more painful. I began to feel abandoned and punished.

I recalled a reading with the Guides in which Merlin told me that I had to let go and learn to accept that some things were beyond me. *What you feel is beyond you and the solution is in further surrender.* He told me that I was expecting the Creator to make my life better, to lift the pain and that is not the Creator's job. He told me that I needed to open my mind and heart and trust that I am on a path that is leading to the highest good.

As I remembered his words, I felt the Creator's love focused on me. For the moment, I was able to be in the present again and not focus on a man or my mother's possible death. The pain lifted and I felt myself becoming my real and true self once again and not a pain-filled creation.

During this time, I was challenged to embrace the two greatest extremes I could ever imagine. On the one hand was the crushing pain of my mother's potential death and on the other, the exquisite beauty of the Infinite Love that was entwining itself with me and shaping my life. Bouncing back and forth like a rubber ball, of necessity I had to learn deeper and deeper surrender.

On Valentine's Day, Shamuki and I were hiking in the mountains admiring the beauty of some flowers when my lower back seized up for no apparent reason. Doubled over in pain, I was unable to even stand upright and literally crawled up the steep incline of my driveway. As I was crawling and stumbling into the house the phone was ringing. It was my father was calling to tell me that my mother had been rushed to the hospital and was failing rapidly. I asked him to put her on the phone.

A thick, groggy voice that was a pale echo of my mother's usual vibrant tones weakly greeted me. "I'm dying, Anamika."

"I'm jumping on the next plane. Don't die before I get there," I implored.

"I'll wait for you, sweetheart," she assured me.

No wonder my body had seized up! I had allowed myself to hope that she was healing. That hope made this violent blow even more devastating. Though I was mentally prepared for this eventuality, nothing could have prepared me emotionally. I went back into that state of numb shock I had felt at the time of my mother's first phone call.

Half of me was in my body and the other half pulled out with my mother who was dwelling more and more in another dimension. I yearned to wake up from this bad dream and return to the joyous life I had been living since my last reading. My spiritual self could feel the beauty, power and opportunity of this transition and could even celebrate my mother's liberation. But my human emotional self was devastated beyond description. The reality of her dying was unspeakable and unbearable. It was beyond my ability to cope with this situation or to accept what was happening.

In addition to being my mother, the most primal, life-giving connection, she was also my soul mate, my deepest love, best friend, trusted advisor and the foundation of my being. We shared everything and understood each other without words. She saw me through the eyes of her soul. We had persisted through many, many years of working out the glitches and all the while she had been there loving me, boosting me up and cheering me on. For the most part, she had supported my path and understood my motives.

Like Yeshua, my mother was my first and best teacher. A powerful, highly psychic and gifted woman, she spread love to all around her. Everyone who knew her considered her to be truly remarkable. During her illness our love had deepened as she became more vulnerable and open to receiving rather than just giving.

During my last visit with her I had sat hour after hour holding her ailing, cancer-ridden body. I looked into her eyes while she was awake. There was nothing left to say but, "I love you beyond all measure, more than life itself and I will always be with you."

I had silently communicated, "I have more work to do here in this world, but I'll join you as fast as I can." She had looked deeply into my soul and repeated to me what she had told me again and again from the day I was born, "How could I ever love anyone more than you?"

All too soon her condition had worsened. Now she was in the hospital and failing rapidly. My child-self wailed and grieved for my mommy and my adult-self held her in my strength as my being cracked, shattered and broke wide open. Whatever traumatic life transitions I had previously experienced paled before the impending death of my mother. It was by far the worst. Nothing could compare.

I saw my attachments to her including my inability to let her go, to let her choose her own path and my own selfish need of her physical presence. I saw all of these things, but that didn't change how I felt. I didn't want to let her go, even though I did want her to be happy and free.

Torn between worlds, I called Mataare in hopes that the Guides could help me. Yeshua told me with loving reassurance that the matter was out of their hands. It was now between my mother and the Creator. He said that if she could let go into the heart of the Spirit of the universe, then she could be happy and find the light. He said that there was only a small chance that she would heal in her current body and that she would need my help to make her transition. He reminded me that the love my mother and I had for each other would always be a bridge across the dimensions.

I hung up the phone knowing that ultimately I would have to walk this alone. While Yeshua's words gave me comfort, I still felt pain searing through my heart and soul, tearing me open until my nerves seemed raw and exposed. I felt helpless and vulnerable to the point of wanting to die with her.

I reviewed our life together and it seemed so unfair for her to die now. I had spent years making my way through the entanglements between us. We had shared those years of darkness and now that our lives were finally opening into joy, I wanted to share that with her too. I wanted to reap the rewards of our hard work together. I was finally becoming my true self, poised on the brink of having my lifelong dreams fulfilled and I wouldn't be able to share it physically with the one about whom I cared most and who cared most about me.

Until now I had not fully appreciated the depth of my mother's love nor seen the radiance and greatness of her Divine Mother spirit. My heart had often been hard and all I had been able to see was my own self-hatred projected outwardly onto her. I had often judged her as lacking, which had caused me great pain.

"Help me forgive myself for this," I prayed. "Mom, please forgive me for every moment I didn't love myself and therefore you, unconditionally. Part of me is dying with you and I pray for rebirth for both of us."

Images of her birthing me and now me escorting her through her death transition flooded me. Death and birth, it's all the same, I mused. I needed help as this was all far beyond me, "Please fill this emptiness and take the angst in my soul. Let me come to know your true love. Help my mother know your true love. I want everything for her. Help me let her go to You. Help me love her with a pure and unselfish heart."

At once I was lifted into another dimension where my mother was dwelling. I saw the magnificence of her spirit and that we were eternally connected. I heard God say, "To enter my heart, you have to let go of everything."

With this understanding, it was now time to face the reality of her impending death and walk it through. I put a brace on my ailing back and hobbled to the airport. I flew to my parents' home by the sea in Connecticut and sat with my mother hour after hour, day after day. She was in and out of consciousness as her breathing became more labored. At night when she would awaken in pain she screamed my name. I jumped out of sleep and ran to her bedside by the picture window overlooking the ocean. The inky black darkness outside felt like it was inside of me. The only light was the illumination that would appear on her face. Periodically, she opened her eyes, smiled weakly at me and then drifted off again.

My family held vigil, suspended outside of time. We functioned as one harmonious organism, taking turns holding her, holding each other, crying in each others' arms, preparing food for each other and talking in hushed tones. Not one element was out of place. It would have been next to impossible to miss the divine orchestration at work around and through us.

Although most of my mother's personality wasn't present anymore, the small part that still remained was experiencing great physical pain despite the ever increasing doses of morphine. I called Mataare again for help and this time it was Merlin who came to my aid.

It is hard for her to hold onto life now and her resistance to death is diminishing. She is transitioning through the dimensions to contact the Supreme today. You will go with her. She will make her decision and come back to inform you of her choice. You have no idea of the power of these moments of being with her. Your heart will forever remain in her soul.

Now listen carefully to my instructions and do this immediately as there is no time to waste. When you are alone with her lie down and hold her feet. See the cancer dissipating. Tell Mataare to light three candles: one black, one blue, and one white, from left to right. Tell him to write her name, Eleanor, and place it under each candle. Next to the black candle he should write, "Cancer gone." Next to the blue one write, "Heavenly inspiration," and next to the white one write, "New life." Then he should offer the candles up to the Creator's Will. There is no time to waste.

Merlin disappeared in haste thrusting Mataare forcefully back into his body and he came to with a groan. When I alerted him to the situation, he said he would channel Merlin again to do the magic as the situation called for extra power. He said he would instruct Merlin to call me when it was done. I agreed and went in to see my mother.

As I entered the room, everyone else mysteriously decided to take a break, leaving me alone with my mother. I breathed a sigh of relief that I didn't have to explain Merlin's magic and I lay down according to his instructions. Very soon I felt a swirling and lifting as I was pulled through the dimensions with my mother. I lost consciousness and awoke with a jolt half an hour later as I was being plunked back into my body. I immediately reached for the phone by the bedside and called my answering service. Merlin's familiar voice had left a message.

Anamika, it is done. We have done our part. Now it is in the hands of the Spirit of the universe. I am with your mother and I shall speak with her. She will be met by some relatives and some of the spirits which will guide her to the light. There with the light her destiny will be chosen. Blessings are with you beloved, and I shall be with you as well.

Later that day I felt myself being pulled out of my body again. I ran back into her room to be with her. For the second time that day, when I arrived the other family members mysteriously departed. My mother and I were lifted through the dimensions and we arrived at the threshold of a door to the light. I was instructed to wait while she was received into the arms of the Supreme Love. While I waited outside the door I could sense the choice that my Mother had made, but I hoped against hope that it wasn't true.

When my consciousness returned to my body, I opened my eyes. As I held her, she stirred and opened her eyes. She looked at me and spoke clearly but from very far away, "Anamika, I want to go home."

The decision had been made. Inwardly, I crumbled but I chose to give her the best of my love, "I know, Mom. It's okay. Go to the light. I will always be with you. We are eternally connected."

She looked at me again from far away and simply whispered, "I know. I love you forever. You are my lover."

I knew what she meant as she spoke to me from eternity. Then she drifted off again as her spirit pulled out and far away. She had that luminous look on her face again.

My mother's lungs were filling with fluid and it was increasingly difficult for her to breathe. I sensed that she was in the last phase and was being pulled out very quickly now. We brought in an overnight nurse who "coincidentally" just happened to be Hungarian, from the old country, as was my mother's mother. How perfect that the guardian of her departure was from the same land as her mother, who was the guardian of her entrance into this world. I asked the nurse to speak to my mother in Hungarian telling her that she loves her and to let go into the light. Seeing her unbearable pain, for her sake, we all sincerely wanted her to let go. As the nurse spoke in Hungarian, my mother turned her head to the nurse and weakly reached her arms toward her as if reaching for her own mother. She relaxed more and drifted farther off.

We were all gathered around her bed. My father was holding her head, I was pressed against her side holding her hand and my sisters and brother were similarly positioned around the bed holding her. Her breathing began to slow and become shallower. Her hands began to get white and grow cold as she was pulling the rest of her life force out of her body.

Her lungs were so filled that she was drowning. Her body was fighting to hold on, struggling to survive, to get air. We gently encouraged her to relax and let go. While it was painful to watch the physical suffering, there was a mystical beauty about it all. I could sense that her spirit was far away. She gasped the word "air," then gradually her breathing lightened until I felt her let go. Then she was gone.

Spontaneous spasms of gut wrenching grief seized up my body and I nearly fell to the floor as my mother pulled stagnant veils off of me and took them with her. She was setting us both free. As the veils tore loose, the psychic and emotional pain were excruciating but it was done. She was returning home, going to where she had chosen to be. A gentle peace spread through my body; it was all okay.

Drawing away from her bed, our arms formed a family circle of love into which we poured our tears, our grief and our pain. We sobbed from the depths of our souls, while in a chorus saying, "It's okay, Mom, head for the light." Our love was the bridge she crossed into the heart of the Divine. I was relieved, yet grief-stricken, held in a protective cocoon of anesthesia-like fog which would wear off at the rate I could handle. We were all walking as if in a dream for space and time had ceased to exist. All I could sense was the most immediate now.

Completion ceremonies arose spontaneously and each was beautiful. We conducted them ourselves, creating them in the moment from the heart. The first one occurred the day after her crossing in a dense bank of fog. We walked out onto the rocks toward the sea with her red Valentine's roses in hand. There was one stem for each person. One by one we gently plucked the red petals and tossed them into the ocean while crying our hearts out. We spoke to her of our love, blessing her on her journey and encouraging her onward. We embraced as a unified group as the petals floated away into the surreal mist.

As always, the elements were in harmony with the mood. The day she crossed there was dense, heavy atmospheric pressure and oppressive overhanging clouds. After she crossed the skies opened up and it poured, mirroring our tears. Then we were fogged in. The ceiling remained low, but the rain lifted as we put her body in the ground. With white roses this time we spoke to her again, one by one placing the flowers on the wooden box before we shoveled in the dirt. One of her friends had brought four chocolate roses wrapped in red tinsel in honor of her love of chocolate.

We invited friends and family to come together later that day to celebrate her life. The sky was beginning to lighten slightly. Holding hands in a large circle, we spoke of her life, told stories, laughed and cried. All agreed that she was no ordinary person. The power and charisma of her Divine Mother love had touched each in a unique way. Such was her gift.

I related the events of the last few days of her crossing and said that I felt that she was doing fine. As soon as the stories were complete there was an audible sigh and we were lifted higher. At that moment the sun burst through the cloud bank for the first time in days. The sky looked like my heart, gray and dense but with rays of light bursting through. We still walked as if in a dream.

Exhausted from the whole ordeal, I lay down to rest and asked God to show me the way. As if a switch were activated, a wellspring of love, like an eternal fountain began to circulate in my heart. My only desire was to share it, to give it away and to let it flow outward, spilling over with grace.

"Ah, this is altruistic love," I thought. "How bittersweet." I was elated and sad. "How ironic," I mused, "to have to lose my deepest love to get more. How true that love is letting go."

I could sense the veils being pulled off gently as I was moving through a tunnel of gray mist. This was my spiritual transition, my mother's parting gift. She had birthed me into this world and I had birthed her into the next dimension. She was carrying me there with her. She and I had midwifed and mothered each other for lifetimes.

She was my true love and would always be. I knew that with her departure from this form my new life would begin. Together we were being birthed into the heart of the Beloved One and were united there forever in our love.

CHAPTER 22

WHEN THE WEAPONS ARE LAID DOWN

It takes great love and great trust to let go and
find out what exists beyond your particular
desire or intention. – Yeshua

In the days after my mother's death, Yeshua helped me to understand and recover.

When your mother entered into a higher dimension where she is now at rest and at peace, there was indeed an exhilaration, great ecstasy, joy and freedom. As she faced the disabling of the ego, she had some resistance, clutching to things of this world to which there was some form of positive or negative attraction. Many fears and emotions surfaced in her spirit, but now she is at rest.

It is said that when the body dies, all that dies is the body but the spirit lives on. That is not entirely true. For indeed something far more than the body is left behind. Within the body are many manifestations and expressions of the psyche, so that when the body dies, vast parts of the psyche die along with it so that the remaining spirit can undergo a powerful and dynamic psychic change.

The change can be so intense and thorough that many times that entity is entirely unrecognizable. There are some souls who entirely resist any sort of change and they suffer greatly. If they indulged in the cultivation of ego, particularly negative ego in the course of their lifetime, they experience a true hell. Resistance to a great and powerful Universal Force requires strong and willful abiding attachment to that which is unreal. Thus, a number of experiences manifest which are completely subject to that entity's own fears or dark side. It is of great advantage to begin letting go of ego and embracing the light long before entering into the higher dimensions at death.

These things are important for you to know, for you are not waiting for your death in order to translate. This translation is the expression of the Creator's love or Will for you. Leaving behind attachments cannot be done as an act of will or intention, but solely by seeking to embrace what you can identify as a loving Creator's intention for you. It takes great love and great trust to let go and find out what exists beyond your particular desire or intention.

This great love or trust comes through the gift of serenity. Through that serenity comes a great and powerful joy which entirely orients one's spirit into a dimension where one is in the same state of being that is embraced at the time of one's translation from the physical world. This is called ascension, enlightenment, or awakening. Ascension is a substantial and vital change in one's psyche such that one is not the being that one was prior to that time.

This is your path, and your mother is a key part of your being able to embrace your next dimension. Do not lose her, but do let her go. Allow her to take whatever form she needs to take, and hold a place in your heart for her to remain forever.

"I do sense veils being removed and I feel detached. It is as if I'm being held outside of space and time. It is a very odd sensation to not be able to relate to anything that is happening on Earth right now."

As you embrace your ascendant nature, problems you experience will be worked out on a spiritual or altruistic plane. Through your own self-honesty and self-examination, as you become aware of this, then ask such things of the Infinite as, "How can I be of optimal service to you? I am open to you to create those shifts in my being and psyche which are necessary that I might be an agent of your light and of great service to you."

Relinquish requests like, "Creator, this is what I need to be of greatest service to you." The slow relinquishing of the focus upon the self is the most fearful surrender of all of humankind. It is the final lifting.

Pain began to fill me, "I am noticing that deep pain and loneliness are surfacing in my chest."

It is the remaining fear that manifests in the form of the belief that if you could somehow control your life you would enjoy it better. In other words, you have tried to make something happen with whatever tools of survival you have, even us. The control is being taken which makes the fear stand clear. That is what you are experiencing. There must be a deep concession in your being that your approach doesn't work.

"No, it doesn't work. I want to surrender the control but I feel desperate and helpless."

Good, with that deep concession, when that pain arises you must prostrate yourself before your God and say, "Take this from me and show me what you would have for me. As frightened as I am about what that might mean, take that fear from me too so I can see it."

Everyone walks with their light side and dark side. When one's dark side is fully accepted, it is disempowered. That is, the charge is taken out of it. Then there is no more fear of any dark side from anyone or anything. Then no person, place, circumstance, or anything external to oneself is a threat to any aspect of one's being. There is no threat when one is comfortable with one's own light and one's own dark. They walk hand-in-hand forward into life.

The shadow self keeps a human being honest, questioning themselves and their nature. The time comes when the shadow self is befriended, when the weapons are laid down and it holds no more strength. The time comes when the shadow self is almost a friend.

Any restlessness, discontent and irritability that may occur from time to time is not because of lack of control over your existence, but rather because of the existing fear within your being. This fear must be finally fully addressed by carrying out your purpose with the intention to serve. Come before your beloved Divine and asked to be saved from the aspects of yourself which are shrouded with fear. You will need to be first willing, then humble enough to be honest with yourself.

You must not delude yourself that somehow you have acquired all that is necessary to have accomplished or achieved any spiritual end. You will have to be honest enough with yourself to see when aspects of your own nature that are in the darkness are currently in operation. Aspects of darkness are things like fear, dishonesty, manipulation, self-centeredness or selfishness. When you see those things creating demands in your being that are not getting addressed, this is what you must ask to be saved from. Don't ask for the fulfillment of those demands; ask rather to be saved from the demand of those demands. Ask to be freed from the burden of those strong desires. Ask to give up those things.

Freedom from these things allows you to live in the light. One gets free by submitting to the Source the instinctual fear-based demands of the will, which drive all motivations towards one's own needs. When one removes these drives by the will of the Divine so that they can serve better, then these things, in the name of their service, are lifted and one begins to know serenity.

In that serenity comes the will being guided by other motivation than the need to survive. Rather, there is a desire to be embraced by the light that one has received, to touch others with that light, and to watch the glow that others have as they too are freed from their inner burdens. This passing on of the light becomes the way one finds freedom.

When I hung up the phone, I fell face down on my belly, sobbing from a deep well of sorrow within myself. "I am utterly helpless and admit that things aren't working. I don't want to be in control anymore. Save me from this aspect of my being. Show me what you would have of me."

As my sobs subsided I felt lighter and was able to go about my day. Suddenly, a strange, ill at ease feeling crept up. Something still wasn't right. In this situation, I would normally use all of the tools and prayers that I had learned. However, something inside me was rebelling. I was sick of doing the right prayer, striving for perfection and getting everything right so that I could "ascend."

Instead of doing it right I said, "You know what, God? If I can't tell you the complete and honest truth about how I feel and if you can't see what's really in my heart anyway, then we have a severe problem in our relationship. I am sick and tired of trying to make myself feel some altruistic love and some ascended state. I am just going to tell you the way I feel. This isn't my highest wisdom or most loving perspective; it's just the emotional garbage at the moment, so here it is. In this moment I don't give a damn about serving! In fact, I don't care about anything or anyone right now.'

It felt good to make these unabashed, honest statements. It felt so good that I persisted: "I want to feel miserable and unhappy. I want to be in control, I want to dictate what's what. In fact, I don't want to give myself to you at all. I want you to bend to MY will. I want to be God!"

Then a dictatorial voice inside of me got really vicious and began to speak: "I want you to be miserable and suffer. I don't want you to even be able to breathe. I don't care about your happiness. I don't care about anybody else's either! I am cold-hearted and don't care about anyone or anything." There was a dispassionate part of me that saw quite clearly that this tyrannical dictator was deriving immense negative pleasure from being in control.

It became startlingly clear that this dictator was blocking my heart from opening further. I had been attempting to force myself to be of service despite this place that didn't give a damn about anything but itself and didn't even care about itself either.

I let the dictator loom so large that it occupied all of the space. Then a gentle, soothing voice came from the deepest recesses of my heart and said to the dictator: *All I want is for you to be happy.*

This genuine caring caught the dictator so off guard that "he" burst into tears. "I didn't know you cared about my happiness. I have never felt this loved unconditionally, just because I exist."

I redirected my words back to God: "I never felt that you wanted me to be happy either. I have felt that you just want me to do the service, the Great Work. I've been resisting on this level because I never felt like you cared about me just for me." Having so said, the dictator crumbled in a deflated heap and disapperared.

After his departure what remained was the gentle voice of God in the center of my heart. There was God, talking to me audibly in conversation: *I care most about your happiness and your control has been in the way of you receiving My love.*

"All I care about is being happy."

Let that desire go too. There's something beyond what you are thinking of as happiness. You don't yet even know the fullness of what I can give you, so don't limit yourself from receiving in any way, or by any belief or definition.

I replied from the most gentle, delicate, tender open heart: "Teach me how to just be. I want you to teach me everything. What I truly want is whatever your heart's desire is for me."

Suddenly a profound joy exploded in my heart. "Oh, this is the God union in the heart of the heart. It's so simple, sweet, gentle and easy." Uncharacteristically, I experienced excitement about the unknown instead of the usual fear. In that moment I knew that God wanted me to experience love infinitely and forever.

I had feared God and attempted to stay in control, bracing against punishment, judgment and deprivation. I had felt, "You're taking away yet another relationship, money or some aspect of my being and I don't experience that as your help. It registers as deprivation and punishment. You must be punishing me because I am so unlovable that I'm supposed to suffer. I will never get what I want, so I had better grab it for myself."

All the while God was lifting me beyond the limitations of what I thought I wanted to a new context I couldn't yet see. "From this place of trust, I let my life go and put myself solely in your hands." I said, "I happily follow whatever you would have of me, because it's so far better than anything I could arrange for myself."

I had never expected to be plunked into the heart of God in this way. I felt God dwelling deep within my heart and I was dwelling in the heart of my Beloved. The Guides had often said that union always occurs in the most unexpected way. As I surrendered control, the old dictator became the liberator. I was entwined with God in a fluid and ever-changing love. The yearning for anything outside of myself dissolved as the inner marriage was occurring between the lover and the beloved. They became One.

I am your lover, the gentle voice inside my heart resumed. An indescribable sweetness surrounded me and once again I felt that unbearably beautiful intimacy I had been craving throughout eternity.

A gentle and tender mist of energy gradually enveloped me. I sensed a luminous presence inside that I knew was God. This presence magnetically somehow drew me into Itself and as I let go into it, I sensed that this was the process my mother had experienced in her transition. Held in this love, I understood why her choice to surrender to it was inevitable. The world held no sway; this love was her home.

It became evident that this attraction had always been present. It was my own limitations in receiving its magnitude that regulated the flow. As I realized that God had always been there drawing me inexorably into Its heart, I dissolved into the tender embrace. Paradoxically, I became both me and we . Simultaneously, I had both merged with and been absorbed into love and utter joy. It was love like no other.

It has been said that there is a review of life when one dies and crosses over. In near death experiences, many have reported that their life flashes before their eyes. A similar review occurred now as if I were physically dying. For hours I watched scenes from my life as if on video. There were childhood scenes of my mother holding me, a physical warmth that I would never feel again from her in this life There were scenes from the past few years, relationships with lovers and on and on. I cried for hours as each scene passed by, saying goodbye to what had been and feeling the loss of my life as I had known it.

As the review came to a close, I was shown several memories again and this time there was no pain. The charge was gone. The scenes were simply memories, filed in the memory bank of life. I attempted to see the future and it did not exist. I looked back into the past. It was complete. Sitting in the vast emptiness of now, with the past released and no future in sight, I breathed a sigh of relief.

"I have nothing left to give you but this self-doubt."

Yes, you do have something more to give me, it's your trust.

These words slammed me against a great wall of fear that was within me. I began to cry as this fear clutched my heart. "I give you my trust. Please take it quickly and don't let me take it back." As I said this, fear of entrapment and suffocation loomed large, threatening to reverse my decision. My lungs tightened making it nearly impossible to breathe.

"Despite this fear, I commit. Don't let me leave you. Don't let me pull away, walk away, or take my love away. Hold me close. Take away my will and let me follow yours. This control has been blocking my full union with you. I commit to commit, despite all fear."

Suddendly, I sensed a presence approach from behind. "In the back door again," I thought. "I'm getting used to how this works." I turned to face the approaching spirit. I couldn't see his face, but as we gently merged I experienced an explosive joy so great that I was washed over with tears of gratitude as I recognized him as my true soul mate. "Oh!" I gasped. "This is what the Guides meant when they said that I would feel undeniable joy when I was with the right one."

CHAPTER 23

PASSION FLAME

There are always crises of trust and faith
as one contacts a deeper level until a certain point.
That point is called a spiritual awakening. – Miriam

Each time I experienced blissful and peaceful states, I thought they would last forever, but they didn't. I could remember those moments so well and imagined experiencing them again. In those moments, everything was fine and nothing else needed to happen. Now, I could imagine them but I couldn't really feel them. Here I was again back in the gut wrenching terror that was consuming me. I must be doing the journey all wrong.

I called Mataare and screamed at the Guides: "The constant non-arrival of my soul mate physically makes me feel there is something wrong with me. No matter how much I adhere to the spiritual path, it never happens. This lack of intimacy makes me feel like I am starving to death and that this is okay with the Creator. Why is it okay that I get sacrificed? It doesn't seem to matter that it has taken all of this time. My deepest pain never gets fully lifted and instead my own insecurities get shoved back in my face. I can't take this any more!

Miriam's infinitely patient voice responded. *We suggest that you stop rejecting other people's love for you just because you don't feel it or understand it. You must make a conscious attempt to receive it deeply as God's love for you if you can't accept it as their love for you. You need to let this love happen now, and have the focus of the monk which is humility through work. Monks love work because it busies and focuses their spirit. Even when they are tired, true monks love work because they love to pack as much as possible into the stream of life so that they are of maximum service to the Supreme.*

There is a reason that none of your soul mates have partnered with you even though they all have desired it. You won't see them. You see instead your own shortcomings and fears. Thus, you want someone that you believe is past the point that you are.

You judge your shortcomings as unworthy and cannot forgive them, so there is not the forgiveness that should be there for the shortcomings of others. Therefore, you are deprived of the love of your soul mates. You must love yourself with your imperfections and let others love you with their imperfect love. You must acknowledge that you can't stand your own shortcomings.

I was still raging at the Guides. "Everything you are saying is true, but I can't do any of this. My helplessness makes me feel even more hopeless because there is not one piece of what you are saying that I can do. You are telling me that I must do this and be like that and I can't do any of it. I don't have the ability. I can't love myself. I can't make myself receive love. I can't be like the monk. I can't enjoy the work or love the process. Right now I hate it all! I don't believe that I will ever be loved no matter how hard I try and I don't trust God!"

You must be willing to let go. When the horror of all those unmet needs and wants occurs as you watch your whole life dying before you, only that willingness will keep you hanging on. The reality that has been a container around your true self dies hard.

You are not supposed to know whether there is a God or not, otherwise how could you be open? If Creator is infinite there's always going to be some unknown part about which one sooner or later must feel some uncertainty. If it is infinite it has to be that way, and if one is open, one has to be open to that possibility. Only if one is closed can one be absolute.

There are always crises of trust and faith as one contacts a deeper level until a certain point. That point is called a spiritual awakening. This is a fight of faith that is given to a person. They haven't earned it but have been open to it. At some point the Great Spirit bestows faith or serenity upon that person so that they can cross the border of the previously unknown, utilizing that quality of trust that has been issued to them. Sometimes it takes going into a deep cavernous place.

"I am in the bowels of hell and don't think I can't survive this one. I feel like I'm going to die right now. I'm suffocating." Wracked with pain, I began gasping for breath. "I need help, I can't breathe. Don't leave me, God, I need you."

That's right, you just did the right thing. "Dear God, hold me now." There it is. From the place deep down, that dead place, from the dying, here is God to fill you right now.

As I felt God's loving presence holding, filling and soothing me, I began to relax. In the embrace of God's limitless love, I could now see that the identity I had constructed as an attempt to try to be something was in fact nothing. I had identified thoroughly with this limited, finite self, hoping it would make me feel worthy. I felt that own naked essence was not enough. To surrender that identity seemed to be the death of me. Althought, it was the identity that was dying and not me, it felt like me. I had invested so much in this persona that I thought was me, that I did not know much of who I truly was. What I thought was really me was in fact a limited, finite self.

I realized that I had not walked humbly with God. In my arrogance and pride, I had created the perceived separation that was causing me so much pain. It was in fact my responsibility, not God's.

As I became aware of this, a thin veil deep inside my heart gently dissolved and I was able to perceive a little ball of light which had been hidden underneath it. As I entered this ball of light, I realized that I was this light. In the beauty of this light, I met the unique aspect of God that is me. Instantly, I fell in love, but this time it was with myself.

I felt this light begin to expand and fill me up. At this point, I felt devastated that it had taken so much time and effort to get to the most simple, profound truth of who I am. Heartbroken, I had to forgive myself for whatever it had taken. As I finally understood that every step of the journey was necessary, a gentle peace descended.

God was winning my heart and trust. I found myself moving my God ring back to the ring finger of the left hand. However, it ended up on the middle finger instead. "Almost but not quite," I heard myself say aloud. I approached God, "I want to marry you anew. I now see that you are the one I have been searching for. It's you that I want and I've been projecting it on a man. You are welcome to bring me one man, many men and anything else of yourself that you choose to give. However the bottom line is that I want to marry you."

I felt myself as a one year old little girl who wanted to marry her daddy. I had buried those feeling under heaps of shame. Wait a minute! Modern psychology has it totally backwards! Of course every child wants to marry their parent because the parent is the child's metaphor for God. "I want to marry you, God. Will you have me?"

God replied, *Yes, but I must prepare you.* I pulled my God ring off of my middle finger and held it above my ring finger.

Are you ready now? This time for real I said "Yes!" and gave my heart. "I don't want You to have to beg for my heart anymore. I joyfully come home and enter Your heart freely and fully." I slid the ring down my ring finger.

Piercing light, ecstasy and love penetrated me as never before. Sensations and emotions opened that I did not even know existed. Entwined in the arms of my Beloved I heard God's gentle voice say, *Do*

I please you as your lover? I melted. "Please me? This is the most exquisite lovemaking I have ever experienced!"

It was so ironic that one conclusion of my search was this: I will never know with my mind if God exists, but I no longer care because I know God from my own direct experience.

I could now answer one of my most important questions: "Is God everything?" "Yes, you are for real, forever and all things. I know this now because I feel helplessly, unreasonably and utterly in love with you." I had crossed a threshold into the light, into the heart of my Beloved. I was wide open in a sea of infinite possibility.

Openness creates a vastness in which to be shown more and more and more and more. Every day becomes the revelation of the spiritual experience. One moves through life happily to the extent that one can embrace faith. Faith does not mean the belief that everything is all right. Faith means an openness everywhere to the spiritual experience.

The Creator has put you in this world for a purpose. That purpose is only realized through surrender. Your ordinary day to day life, which is based upon survival oriented needs, cannot be arranged according to your intellect's capacity of how it should be arranged. Those who open to the higher dimensions need a new power to guide them through existence. Trust is what connects you to that new power. This is what is developing in your being and explains what is going on in your life. A confidence grows from being so honest and true to the self that one comes to see how the universe is working for them. You are the Jewel of the Nile, beloved one.

A space gently opened in the center of my heart. I looked inward and saw there a beautiful shining jewel. Inside the jewel was a flame, a passion flame. It was emanating a radiance so bright and so pure that tears of joy slid down my cheeks. "Ah," I thought, "This is who I truly am. This is the Jewel of the Nile. Each one of us is a unique, magnificent jewel emanating our radiance. This is the context of that other dimension of which the Guides spoke. Within this context the highs and lows could come and go, but they did seem small and irrelevant.

I began to trust life as it unfolded. This state of being had a peace, an acceptance and a calm that was nothing like what I had I previously expected. I was forced to throw away the images I had held of enlightenment and of my future life to simply be in the unfolding now.

One by one I took the dreams I had constructed for my life and tossed them into the sea with rose petals like when my mother had crossed over. The very largest petals were the dreams of a future unnamed man. I watched as the mist surrounded the petals and the waters gently carried them away.

This radiance persisted, and as it did I found myself becoming enraged. I was enraged that I had never believed that I had the right to exist simply as myself. I was enraged that I had been referencing life and God outside of myself. I was enraged that I had never felt that my existence was valid.

As I dared to claim my validity, my own life force explosively surged through me with a sweetness I had never before experienced. In this surge, I experienced not only a personally intimate union with God, but validity as myself and my right to express myself fully as me. In this sweetness, I realized that I was not searching for a man; I had been searching for myself.

Over the next few weeks a cocoon formed around me. Burrowing deeply inside it, the outer world dropped away to such a degree that I could barely even speak. Oddly, my physical body seemed to be dying. My skin turned gray and my mane of black curls fell out in handfuls. At first I was horrified, then I jokingly referred to my ailment as Old Soul's Syndrome because even my physical body had to be remade anew.

The dying intensified and I revisited the symptoms of childhood illnesses as they were exorcised. It was as if the plug had been pulled and I was drained of all of my vitality.

Physically exhausted, I moved from the couch to the chair and back to the couch again. These short trips across the room required every bit of energy. Dishes piled up in the sink and dust settled throughout the house as all of my physical energy was of necessity focused on this transformation.

I came to understand that I was doing was akin to reincarnating in the same physical body without literally dying and having to come back again. My old life purpose was complete and the old programs had dropped away. My only purpose now was being and becoming. I was living in a still point, a null zone. Nothing outside of this zone existed as I allowed myself to be made anew.

The null zone lasted for three days, paralleling the time frame of Yeshua's resurrection. During that time, I experienced myself physically dying, crossing a border and then coming back to life again. On the morning of the fourth day I sprung awake at 5 am full of life energy and joy. My body was ravaged by the ordeal but I saw that I now had the resources to begin the process of rebuilding.

With trust in this unknown process, I gave the care and sustenance of my body over to God. Instead of me breathing, I let God breathe me in and out of creation. Something other than me was breathing me back into life. My DNA was being recalibrated, rewired and re-encoded to a higher frequency.

Surprisingly, my life until this moment now seemed like a past life of my present self. I had lived that old life in a different dimension of being. That life had been a struggle to get somewhere, to become who I truly knew myself to be.

Now, I was aware of being connected to God deep within with no gripping thoughts of a soul mate and no angst of the soul. There was nothing other than living love, which was simple, harmonious and splendid. My life in this new dimension of being was beginning to unfold.

In the midst of these wonderful changes, Shamuki developed an oozing, infectious tumor on the underside of a toe on his left rear paw. I had it biopsied and it proved to be malignant. The vet recommended amputation of the toe and possibly the entire leg. I was totally shocked. Losing even a toe was beyond imagination. Losing a leg was even worse and losing him all together was more than I could endure.

Unable to be objective, I desperately sought the counsel of the Guides. They assured me that Shamuki was not ready to leave his body. He was going through his own clearing, they explained. Through this process, he was aiding my own liberation.

I decided that the only way to deal with any of this was to open my arms and invite life in. "Bring it on, if I die, I die. If I live, I live. It's all the same." I proclaimed to the mountains: "I will live life on its own terms, naked, raw, vulnerable, passionate and free! I will no longer live in terror. Thank you, fear, you have taught me about life."

The day of Shamuki's surgery arrived and I awoke ready to face whatever occurred. Shamuki might lose a toe, a foot or a leg. The vet hadn't been able to fortell whether the malignancy had spread or was contained so she had agreed to be guided by her intuition as to how much to remove. I needed to accept whatever outcome was necessary. Taking a deep breath I closed my eyes. I could hear God's voice speaking to me: *I am here for you and with you in every little movement of life. Our sacred trust is growing.*

Out of the mist Yeshua appeared: *Shamuki is an aspect of me sent to remind you and teach you. His work in this way is done as my work with you in this way is done. You and Shamuki and you and I will go on in a new way filled with joy and serenity. He has done his job well. This surgical procedure is his right of passage as well as yours. Celebrate him as this is a graduation for both of you. Stay open minded as well as open hearted and you will see Truth. This is your liberation.*

God and Yeshua were with us and it was time to leave for the vet. Shamuki said he was ready and looked quite peaceful and happy. When we arrived at the clinic I looked at my watch. It was 9 am, November 19th. Then, what hit me like a thunderbolt was that with the time difference between the East and West coasts, it was exactly one year ago today at this exact time that the Call to Healing for my mother had occurred. Here we were, a year later to the very moment, doing it again!

The energy of Sakkara and the spirits of the many people around the country who were participating in Shamuki's rite of passage filled the vet's office. The vet, Gabriella and I held hands around Shamuki. I blessed the vet, asking that she be guided through the surgery and that this sacred ceremony be for everyone's awakening.

The vet smiled and took Shamuki off to begin the surgery. The intensity of Sakkara's penetrating energy and my own fear mingled in my body so strongly that I began to collapse. Gabriella caught me and gently lowered me into a nearby chair.

Staying attuned to Shamuki, I could feel the anesthesia enter his body. He descended into the darkness gathering the collective malignancy to him. Then he pulled it up through the dimensions into the light and went into the heart of God. Once again, as I had done with my mother, I stayed outside the door and waited for him.

As Shamuki was peacefully held by God, I suddenly felt a searing pain in a toe of my left foot. I knew that the vet was cutting his toe at that moment. The pain was excruciating. Suddenly it stopped and my foot felt numb. I could still follow the procedure, but with no pain. Later the vet told me that as she began to cut his toe she noticed that he was experiencing pain so she had increased the gas. She had paused often to listen to her intuition during the operation and Shamuki lost only one toe.

While I was tracking Shamuki, I sensed that I was undergoing surgery as well. Layer by layer, a thick coconut husk of fear was removed from me. As it was sliced away, what remained was my core. This paring of me completed as his surgery came to a close.

As he was reentering his body, a bright beam of light pierced through the top of my head, activating my pineal gland. I could feel the pineal pulsing first a gold, then a white, then a colorless light. That light made its way down my body activating the entire endocrine system gland by gland and filling my body with a new ebullience.

When it was complete, I had been irrevocably changed. The human emotional highs and lows had been cut away. I felt a serenity and compassion that were exquisite and ordinary all at the same time. It was as if I had settled into my home within myself, to the most simple and natural place I had always known. I desired only what was occurring in the moment as nothing else mattered. Each moment, whatever it brought, was my true lover.

Soon after Shamuki's surgery the Guides told me they needed to pull away for a time. Had this occurred earlier, I would have been badly shaken but at this point in time it felt right. The past year had stripped me down to bare bones and I was so naked that there was nothing standing in the way between me and the Beloved One inside myself. I had no semblance of an outer life, only my inner eternal communion with God, the greatest gift of all.

I felt I had the love in my life for which I had searched and it was growing rapidly every day. I took the outer events as evidence of God's love, rather than as validation of my being because in love, I was valid just because I existed. There was nothing to prove anymore. Love was all that mattered.

This love was sweet beyond compare. Some days it was passionate, even erotic as it surged through my body. Other days I smiled and laughed at the play of it all. Tears of gratitude ran down my cheeks for the incomparable beauty and almost unbearable intimacy of its embrace. Truly, there was no way to describe it. Several years ago Yeshua had described his God union as a passion beyond all comprehension. I was beginning to truly understand what he had meant.

As I grew stronger and more sure-footed in this love, gaining confidence in its enduring nature, I was able to let go more deeply into it. Every belief I held about myself, the world, or the nature of reality was gently brought to my attention so that I could go beyond its limitations. Every feeling, even a most exquisite one, had to be surrendered so that something beyond it could emerge. The only consistent thing was a constant letting go and opening into an ever growing appreciation for life.

After several months I felt an impulse to connect with the Guides again. My heart swelled as I felt Yeshua coming through Mataare to be with me.

At this point in your God union you are determining your own sovereign sense of style. When you are satisfied that you are living in the way that best suits your being, you will move back out into the world, but this time in a new way. This time, the way you engage with the world shall be from your spirit and not from your ego. You are poised on the brink of this shift.

You cannot go there by yourself. Even though you have been ready for a long time, intuitively you decided to wait until there were enough people ready to go with you. If you went alone, others would not benefit from your union. You are waiting until there is a readiness amongst those you were sent here to help.

You have an instinctive awareness about when the time is right. This awareness could cause a great impatience in your psyche, torturous pain and even hatred for your position in the world. But that would only occur if you lose awareness that you are also one with those who are not yet ready as well as one with those who are ready. Remember, "I am they too as they are me." You stand on the very edge of the cliff in faith and trust until the final moment that others too may be brought through the doorway. Your faith is holding the doorway open to go through for you have come as a pioneer and guide.

You have come here with the awareness that humankind is in a dire condition. The urgency of the current opportunity for humankind to change collects in your psyche as it did in mine. It collected in the soul of every great Master who has come into this world. These Master souls are like saviors to those who would cross the border from darkness into light. It is put into the mind of such Masters to reach with a passion to the light and to arouse that passion in others. The Master gives the others a gift of light by the grace of that one who can see.

This is not an easy task. This is why you are sent reminders and support to keep you able to do the work you came here to do. You find little other reason for existence except to carry the light, and you would be satisfied with no less than carrying the light to the ultimate degree.

Surrender is what makes you beautiful to others. When that surrender happens each time, you suddenly become accessible to others. Then their support is immediately rushed to you. By your surrender to the Creator, it creates a tremendous beauty which is compelling to others and it is from that beauty that your soul mate relationship is born.

Be careful however, for since this tremendous and beautiful power is now at hand, there will be numbers easily drawn to you. You could quickly find yourself in old familiar territory. So difficult was this energy for me to manage that it took me to past sixty years old to have a mate. Every time I drew near to that point I had to withdraw for it became beyond my ability to manage. When the time came that I finally took a mate, I could not believe that it wouldn't be one more complicated situation. Then I received that relationship and it lasted the whole of my life.

All through that relationship I remembered every other relationship which had almost begun. I wished I could have somehow been more ready. I never got to a point where I saw the perfection in the past. I only got to the point of appreciating the perfection of the now. To this day, I still do not see the personal perfection of the past, but I appreciate it because it helped me arrive where I am now.

You have similar feelings and I wish to validate them. You must know that this is how it is for Masters, and it's all right. Notice the signs of these attractions around you and with them their complexities, but fear not. In resolving those complexities in creating holy and sacred relationships, you will develop the subtle finesse that is indescribable. You are positioning to draw in the true soul mate partner. And miracles will result in the lives of all who come close to you as well as in yours. Eventually, you will be seen as the grandmother of a vast and great good. Continue to embrace your destiny gently, great one. We love you, we honor you, we revere you and we shall guide you every step of the way.

I sat breathlessly absorbing Yeshua's words. There was nothing left to say. All that mattered was that my heart was bursting open with ever more love day by day.

The way your mind was holding the dream or the quest will never be. The quest is over. The dream is done. Smash the cup of the holy grail and allow yourself to be fully absorbed into the formlessness.

CHAPTER 24

SHAMUKI'S GIFT

There comes a time when all you know
is love absolutely and there's no fear of anything. – God

Strange news arrived regarding Shamuki's toe. The vet had sent the malignancy off to the lab for analysis and the report came back saying that the kind of malignancy he had developed could be found only in humans.

He healed beautifully after his toe amputation. As his energy returned, he was as vital as ever. Then a year later, out of the blue, his entire body was riddled with cancer. And once again, he was dying.

During this time my own fatigue had become worse again and my body was failing again also. I was extremely weak and my endocrine system was shutting down. I spent most of my time lying inert on the couch, physically unable to move.

Shamuki was weakening rapidly as I was attempting to regain my strength. I had not been able to mean it sincerely when my mother was crossing, so I tried get it right this time. "It's okay if you need to leave," I eeked out. But I knew I was lying. I had to get more honest about how I felt. I approached him guiltily, certain I was doing it all wrong yet again. "Shamuki, I don't feel okay about you dying. You might not care about your body being full of cancer, but I do. Do you think it's okay for you to die and leave me here on my own? You're my partner and this is not okay with me!" There, I had said it.

"I understand how you feel," he replied gently. "And you're right, I do not place the same value on my body or staying in physical form that you do. I came here to serve you and the world. I have served you by taking on a dog form because we are soul lovers and you wouldn't have been ready to have this level of intimacy with a man. You would have projected all of your personal relationship needs and demands onto me if had I been human. The only way I could get my love through to you was by being in a non-threatening form so you could open your heart to me."

He also pointed out that I was too attached to form and that it would serve me to surrender that attachment. As he said this, I realized that much of my effort to save Shamuki from his cancer was an attempt to not face my own fear of loss.

I was too attached to his warm furry body as a source of comfort, safety and security. I wanted to control the outcome of his life to calm my own fears and meet my own needs. Like with my mother's passage, I came to realize that what was important was not whether Shamuki stayed or left in physical form. It was about giving it all to God and trusting the higher wisdom of the dance that was occuring with Shamuki.

While I could find this spiritual perspective, like with my mother, my human emotional nature was strained beyond belief. As I faced the prospect of Shamuki dying, it was as if my lover and partner were dying. Bereft, it was during an episode of gut-wrenching sobs that I felt my heart and soul literally torn like a fabric. I felt I wasn't going to survive and couldn't handle this degree of devastating loss. This was especially true in the wake of my mother's recent death. I asked that I be given the strength to put Shamuki's well-being above my own pain. I asked for the courage to align with whatever he most needed.

As I prayed for help, I sensed myself being ripped apart again. Then I felt something like a balloon blowing up inside of me, filling me with love while weaving the torn fabric into a beautiful new fabric that was full of love for Shamuki.

In this new place, I could now care about his well-being and blessedly there was no room for anything else. Some new form of relationship between us was being created, whether it was physical or not. I needed a continuous miracle to trust this dance with Shamuki to come to lasting peace with a change of form if he died. Something about our scenario also strangely reminded me of the little I knew of Isis and Osiris.

Isis and Osiris were twins, wife and husband, and the Queen and King of Egypt, which flourished under their rule. According to the myth, their brother Sept killed Osiris in a jealous rage, cut his body into fourteen pieces and scattered them around the land. Isis went all over Egypt collecting the parts of Osiris. She found all but the phallus, which had been eaten by a crocodile.

Isis put Osiris back together and as such he was re-membered. Then she fashioned a golden phallus for him and became impregnated. Their son, Horus, known as the savior, became ruler of Egypt and the land once again became rich and abundant. Theirs is a story of the journey from duality to unity. The twins, the beloved ones, faced separation, death and resurrection, remembered who they were and created a new and more awakened entity from the union of the two.

The story of Isis and Osiris resonated deeply within me. Isis came to me often in Sakkara. Also, when the Guides spoke to me through Mataare, she was the primary female voice who often came blended with Miriam. I often felt Isis in my body as she instructed me in healing practices and worked with others through me. People constantly brought me Egyptian drawings of Isis on papyrus and statues of her. These images triggered passionate as well as painful memories of her life with Osiris. Whenever I met men who had an aspect of Osiris' soul, these were the ones to whom I was powerfully drawn.

One day, in response to my prayers for help regarding Shamuki's cancer, I was impressed to take him down to the mountain stream near my house. I bundled Shamuki into a warm blanket in the back seat of the car. On the way there, Isis jumped into my body: *I am Queen Isis. I am here to come back into sacred union with my beloved Osiris. Our spirits are blending and we ready to come back as one.*

When we arrived at the stream, Shamuki and I slowly made our way over slippery rocks to a small waterfall running into a pool of very clear, cold water. I sat on a jagged but dry rock next to the pool as he paddled in the refreshing water. Isis instructed me to cup my hands and put water first on Shamuki's head and then on his tail. As I was putting water on his tail I heard her chant the incantation: *Cancer be gone. It's time for the burdens to be lifted. Cancer be gone.*

I was instructed to put water on top of my own head as well. *Fear of loss be gone.* My eyes were closed as the cold water was gently dripping down my face. Suddenly, I sensed my spirit begin to blend with Shamuki's and we were entwined as one spirit. When I opened my eyes, Shamuki's nose was very close to my face and he had put his wet muddy paw on my sweatshirt directly over my heart. He was gazing deeply into my eyes. I kissed him on the nose and put my forehead against his in acknowledgment that a merging between us had taken place.

"Shamuki, may your burdens be released. May you choose whatever is your heart's desire."

I suddenly felt a dark spot in my sacrum where Shamuki's cancer was lodged, and a piercing pain ran down my leg. "Shamuki, let go of the pain of the world. You don't need to sacrifice your body to help heal the world. If you want to leave you're free to go, but let go of the pain of the world."

Shamuki's cancer once again disappeared almost instantaneously and we were able to enjoy a brief, blissful interlude. I recognized the Isis/Osiris archetype I was playing out with Shamuki. He would get cancer and we would resurrect him, then the whole process would start over again. We had done this dance a few times already. I felt I had to stop putting a priority on resurrecting his form, because his life was not up to me. Shamuki and I were blended as one in spirit and I needed to trust the perfection of his choices.

My ability to put his needs above my own was a miracle for me. While I had believed the rightness of this way of being in theory, I had never been able to actually do it. I had always before been able only to aspire to this kind of acceptance. It's what the Guides referred to as altruistic love. In this kind of love I cared so much for Shamuki's well-being that I truly wanted what was best for him. This kind of love took me beyond my own fears.

If people were to fully understand the grace of what awaits them they would never fear life or death again, for the fear of life is as strong as the fear of death. The fear of the light is as strong as the fear of the darkness. There comes a time when all you know is love absolutely and there's no fear of anything. You are at that juncture now and so is your friend Shamuki. Allow him to rest here in my love. Life is not difficult when you let my hand carry you and when you do not attempt to orchestrate life for yourself from your own limited vantage point. Let me show you the way.

I surrendered Shamuki's journey to God and was beginning to grow a little stronger physically when his cancer came raging back. Shamuki was now seriously ill and stopped eating. With each passing day we were marching closer to his death.

Masters often willingly take on some of the karma of those they are here to help. This manifests frequently as cancer and this has happened with Shamuki. You should not assume that he is taking on your own karma exclusively or to such an extent that it is killing him. For he has worked not only with you in the higher planes while he was here, but with many people you do not even know as well as many of those you do. His body is close to the point where it can no longer hold all that he has taken on and therefore he anxiously awaits his next level and his new way of showing you who he is.

"What I see when I look into his eyes is the greatest love I've ever known. All I ever see looking back at me is a love that only has concern for my well being. I don't know how to be here without him."

Since Shamuki is your longest intimate, the lesson here is most extraordinary, most powerful and most difficult to come to terms with. The more intimate you become with any being, the more powerful the lesson. Shamuki's surrender to his process of transitioning is most challenging to you for you are going through that transition as well. It leaves you out of control of whether his destiny shall take him one way or another, healing physically or transitioning from this place.

This is a most extraordinary challenge and as he goes back and forth between manifesting cancer and then healing it, he loosens his grip on his direction and destiny. He embraces his surrender to the truth. You too are experiencing literally being pulled back and forth, twisted, jerked and turned asunder by the process, which the intimacy with him brings about. That is the purpose of what he is going through with regards to you. He is giving you a precious gift of facilitating a deep ability to let go and allow an intimate to fulfill and express their own destiny in their own way while you become unconditionally accepting of that.

A great obstacle with regards to relationship has been accepting an intimate for who they are, not what you see them as being able to become or not become. Since this is a vital part of relationship for you, going through this experience also opens the door to allowing relationship to manifest in an abundant and rich manner.

Shamuki rapidly arrived at what seemed to be the end. I took him outside under the full moon and lay curled up around him, certain he was going to cross that night. When he dozed, I dozed. He was very far from his body and I felt him go to God. Just as with my mother, I had to stay outside the door. He entered and communed with God and I felt he was just going to cross at that point. He was merged with God and like with my mother, I knew he had decided it was time to go home.

When the sun broke at five a.m., Shamuki surprisingly came back into his body, jumped up off of his deathbed and said, "I feel great. I want turkey breast, peanut butter and cheesecake." I was so relieved he was alive that I didn't question his food selections. I hopped into the car and drove to the store to buy him turkey breast, peanut butter and cheesecake. He wolfed it all down. "I feel great, better than ever!" he proclaimed. The cancer was completely gone and once again he'd had an absolute miracle healing.

I thought optimistically, "Finally, the death cycle is over. He'll be here now." Then he said to me, "You have to understand, besides being an aspect of Osiris, I'm also an aspect of Yeshua. I've come to train you, to teach you, to guide you and to love you. Yeshua went through his death and resurrection and right now, I'm following in Yeshua's tracks."

Realizing he was going to go through some kind of amazing ascension process, I could do nothing but experience it along with him. Shamuki was in a state of absolute grace for six days. He emitted a golden glow and radiated a colorless light that surrounded him entirely. There was not a sign of any illness, just the most ascendant and blessed state I had ever witnessed.

Thankfully, Merlin came to speak to me, as I was craving some perspective on these events. *You find yourself brought to this juncture by your spirit traveler Shamuki who has now fully accomplished what he came to Earth to do. He came to awaken the readiness of your own human heart and to have the very human experience of serving a greater master. For that is indeed the revelation of all of the great Avatars who walk upon the planet no matter in what age or with whatever particular purpose they have come. There is one truth that has been known to all of them and that is that they have come to serve something greater than themselves. Regardless of what level of knowing they are able to manifest in the world, they still always acknowledge the edges of their knowing. They give way to the great mystery. They give way to that which they serve.*

That surrender brings them into a station in the heart where they begin to simply channel love. Love for the sake of love because love is the carrier wave through which the mystery rides. All things in revelation, all things that can be known are carried on the wave of love. And that, my dearest, is in fact a part of your own realization.

It is coming to you in a wave that is being carried through your body and is being nurtured by your own emotional expression as you allow your heart to break and expand that part of your being. Allow the movement of awareness to flow through you. Then, when the moment arrives and you find yourself in front of another who needs to hear something or who needs to be touched in a certain way, you can, even not knowing exactly how to do it, simply let go to the moment and let the wave do it through you. It is the wave and not you that is acting, the wave and not you.

Together we were in a sea a love riding the waves until the morning of the seventh day when Shamuki had a violent seizure that woke me up. He said, "This is the day I have to go. I didn't want to have to ask this of you, but I need your help. I couldn't quite let go of my physical form and now I'm in terrible pain. I have to go and today is the day."

Stunned because he had no cancer so I had erroneously assumed he was staying, I complied with his needs. I called the vet and my closest friends so that we could perform a ceremony to help him leave. Shamuki was totally ready to go and he fervently wished to be released from his body. He asked that I smudge inside the house and a circle around the house with white sage to purify the environment for his departure. He wanted everyone to know that he was absolutely at peace and ready to go. "Let's just be together and be full of joy at the wonderful life that we have had together. This time is done, so let's go forward from here."

Gabriella and several other friends come over quickly. She draped a Tibetan shawl around Shamuki's neck. For the final time I lay down beside him, wrapping my body around him. As I looked deeply into his eyes first I saw Osiris, then Yeshua and then God. In a flash, I finally understood who Shamuki really was. He was God incarnate in dog form and he was an aspect of my truest love.

Your friend Shamuki and you have existed at various points in your world and not least of your remembrance takes place in the land that you have referred to as Egypt. There Shamuki existed not just as Osiris but as the Rain Goddess, who supported the growth of crops and food stuffs surrounding the Nile Valley. You and Shamuki were one as the Rain Goddess and split apart into Isis and Osiris to know each other.

It's time for the fragments to be brought into union. Not that they'll be lost, for you will still have access to the individuality of the fragments, but in their union they become alchemized into a new configuration. Then, some new form will be revealed that is different and beyond anything that you can presently imagine. Allow the container of your current relationship to be shattered.

As I heard these words, I sensed the vet approaching us with the needle. I clutched my furry friend's ailing body helplessly against my chest. "Shamuki, I can't do this." He was lying there in a state of total peace and was quite weak by now. With great effort he raised his head, licked me all over my face and looked deeply into my eyes. "I love you beyond all measure." He gently lay back down sighing, "I'm ready to go now."

I desperately beseeched the heavens, "Give me courage to do this. Take from me my attachment to Shamuki's form. I offer this attachment to you with this supreme sacrifice of Shamuki's body. I offer these bonds of attachment for transmutation so that true and pure experience of eternal and infinite love can be given. Please set me free to be who I am and to spread the light. Help me now because I can't let him go. He's been so beautiful to me in his form as well as in his spirit. I find myself unable to let go of his form and yet I must. He has asked for liberation and so do I."

Shamuki replied, "There is no separation between us. Remember that I am with you always. Our journey is continuing; I am not leaving you. I am inside of you now, I am next to you and all around you and we have merged as one. Even though it's hard for you to let go, I need your help to do this so I can be set free. I'm not leaving you except in this form and I'm coming to you in a more beautiful and powerful way. You can't yet imagine how we'll be together. Please stay open to being shown."

I had to do it; I had to let go. It took everything I had to turn to the vet and nod to go ahead. I held Shamuki as she put the needle in his vein and he instantly stopped breathing. Shamuki's spirit rose high up in the air above our heads and all of us could see the huge heart he formed in the sky. His liberation resounded loudly through the heavens; "I'm free! I'm free! I love you! I love you! Love is the Universal Energy. The meaning of my name is who I am. I am totally united with the Divine. I am pure love, I am pure joy, I am pure light. I am free in this light. Let yourself be lifted up. Feel the exquisite flower that you are deep in your beautiful heart. You are my heart and I am your heart. This heart which is us is now spread into the infinite heart of God. I am that holy light of love."

Then, I felt Shamuki merging with me. Like a waterfall, the essence of him first sprinkled and then poured itself into my body. Isis and Osiris became one, Shamuki and I became one and God and I became one. I lay there for the longest time wrapped around his inert physical body while his spirit wrapped itself around and through me. I felt myself go with him and my physical presence had lost all meaning. All that mattered was being in that love with him.

Gabriella slowly stood up and indicated that she would take his body to be cremated. Even after his body was gone, the entire house was filled with the essence and fragrance of Shamuki. The house and I were imbued with that luminous glow of the colorless ray. I expected to be in the most horrific grief imaginable with a gaping hole in my heart. Miraculously, it simply wasn't there. Somehow I had been graced with the sublime peace that is God's gift.

While I missed his physical form, I was simultaneously in the deepest grace I had ever known. Clearly, he had taken with him something in me that needed to go and had left me his essence in exchange. This love was so exquisite that it took away the pain.

Although at times I still dreamed of being with him, smelling him, running my fingers through his fur and feeling his silky tongue on my cheek, I sensed a rightness about what had occurred. With each passing day, Shamuki continued to open my heart more and more deeply from within.

Instead of everything being stripped away as it had been before, I was being awakened to a new essence of divine love. Shamuki had paved the way for me. He went through his ascension process and I went through an ascension of the heart through him. I became the "we" that is God and me together.

Daily life became a steady flowering and opening while continuously letting go. I was being shown on a moment by moment basis what was falling away and simply had to allow it. The suffering had ended and the pain had gradually lifted. I had never before experienced life without suffering. What began to replace it was exactly what the Guides had spoken of from miraculous synchronicities to gratitude, relaxed peace and an inexpressible fullness and joy.

What had been challenges became opportunities to embrace more love almost instantaneously. I could now see that my resistance to life had caused my suffering and I didn't experience that kind of resistance anymore. I welcomed life each day as the miraculous and awesome mystery that it was. Each experience became an opportunity for deeper love, greater acceptance and increasing awe about the grand orchestration. What was left was a goodness which constantly got better and better.

In order to embrace love properly, lay aside your vision or fantasy of love as though it were your worst enemy. Say, "All right God, whether you gave me this vision as a gift or whether I hold it as some delusion I need for my fear I cannot tell. But I lay this aside so that you might reveal to me something beyond what I presently understand.

Lay aside the vision you have and see what the Creator will reveal to you. If you need love from a person, embrace love. But you can only embrace it if you lay aside the dream you have held. Know this also, that human love can never fulfill you. Only God can fulfill you. Accept what God has given you externally in human form for now and continue to find the depth of the beauty in the Creator. If this brings you pain when you say, "But why would not God give me that which would fulfill me completely?" I say, the day will come when you thank God for never giving you completely that which fulfills you from the outside so that you may know the Infinite within. Then, the outside becomes something inexplicably beautiful.

The truth is great beyond measure and understanding. The truth has its own course and direction. It is manifesting in your life now all towards the good. Your karma is complete. What is occurring now is a change in your very being so that you can embrace the truth day by day, week by week and year by year to greater and greater extents. There is nothing to be done other than witness and learn. Continue to appreciate that all is good. You are in the flow of divine love and that is all that there is.

I glanced over at a card that I had kept as a symbol of my dream with a man. It had been sitting on my desk for over ten years. On the outside of the card was a beautifully colored drawing depicting two lovers entwined as one. Inside was a quote from Rumi's timeless widom. "Lovers don't finally meet somewhere. They're in each other all along."

It's time for you to lay aside all seeking of the dream outside of you. You can do this now because you have come to know that you and your true lover have indeed been in each other all along.

I picked up the card and carried it to the end of the cliff near my house where the mountains meet the sea. Looking out from this precipice, I felt like I was standing on the edge of eternity. With nothing left to hold onto, I filled my lungs to capacity with the intoxicating air, flung my arms wide open and tossed the card into the wind. As of that very moment, I knew that my lifelong search for the man and the mission had ended. At last, the truth of love was alive within me. And although I can't tell you exactly how it happened, I had been carried across the threshold of eternity into the heart of the Beloved.